The PURSUIT

THE TRUTH THAT WILL
SET YOU FREE IS THE TRUTH
THEY DON'T WANT YOU
TO KNOW

DAVID NORRIE

BEYOND
PUBLISHING

New York | Los Angeles | London | Sydney

This book is dedicated to my wife Angelike and our three girls
With special acknowledgment to my friend and spiritual
brother Kerry Moss

TABLE OF CONTENTS

PREFACE

I pray this book will provide a preparation for your future and armor to the spirit of all who read it. I hope that the words which follow serve as a reminder that our greatest resource, our greatest weapon against those things which come up against us in life on a daily basis, is the infallible WORD OF GOD.

First and foremost, I need to tell you that I'm not a preacher or pastor. I've never been to any seminary or religious school. What I am, is like David of the Bible, a man after God's own heart.

I wrote this book because the world needs two things more than anything; more happy people and more people who take personal responsibility for their happiness. And I know happiness and prosperity are what you seek, because while everybody's story is different, all of them share so much in common.

How do I know this?

I know this because I know stories. My entire adult life I've been a journalist and storyteller. I've listened to people tell me their adventures and pitfalls, their achievements and their perils. It was my job to take their stories and retell them in newspapers and magazines. As the world evolved, newspapers and magazines became relics, so I pivoted and began to use my storytelling skills by applying them to the world of business and entrepreneurship, where I coached both corporations and individuals on how to tell their stories better in order to grow and prosper.

Writing this book is a considerable risk for me. Would I offend or inspire people? I had to make a choice. Do I fill it with fluff and amicable thoughts that everybody would applaud or do I go bold and challenge people? I know where there is no risk, there is no reward but the reward I'm seeking is not mine, but the Lord's by way of stewarding my intention to uphold his Word. So, on one hand, I ask for your patience and understanding and on the other, I ask for your humility and reflection.

At this moment in time, I feel as if a lot of people are lost. We're LOST as a people! Meaning we simply don't have the right directions. We continually tell ourselves that happiness is just around the corner if we could only find love, land the job, or have our candidate elected to office. We need to find more than that. We need to find peace.

I'm here to help you define what it means to be prosperous from a biblical perspective. More importantly, I'm here to help you and your story by telling you more about the most important story ever, that of the one true God.

The most popular definitions of prosperity involve success, money, and possessions. Sure, that's part of it, however, we see that our happiness as a culture isn't up to par with our physical riches. Addiction, abuse, and even suicide touch even the wealthiest of the wealthy. Why? Partly because we've been deceived. Our definitions of success and prosperity have been twisted, contorted, and hijacked by those who don't follow a heavenly God, but earthly ones. We're running toward the wrong end zone to use an old football term.

I invite you to open this book with a new outlook, a new way of understanding and as a way to decipher some of culture's misconceptions about God, his Word and prosperity. By constructing a life with the truth of the Word, you will see with new eyes and listen with new ears to the definitions and stories that were clearly given for us to know, in order that we would have a better relationship with God the father and to find what true prosperity means.

FOREWORD
BY JOEL BROWN

You hear this saying self-sabotage quite often. I actually don't believe it. I don't believe self-sabotage is actually a thing. I think it's an excuse at best. It's a label. The reason why I don't believe it is because I believe that we're always getting what we want.

The question is, which part of ourselves is getting it. The unconscious wants to keep you safe while the conscious really wants those big dreams to come true, right? A lot of what we're hiding, avoiding, and pretending not to know, may in our life show up as little subtleties, little nudges, little whispers of wisdom, a little "go for it", a little "you can do it," right? But because the emotion is more powerful than the thought of you achieving your dream, you fall back into that place, the one of safety and comfort just dreaming right?

In order to change the thought and change the direction, we must have an emotion that's more powerful than that thought or a thought that overrides that emotion.

Enter God.

I believe that God wants us focused on him and his word. He wants us to operate in the higher brackets. He designed us. He created us. He walks with us in hopes that we move into power.

Most people aren't operating in power. They're operating in force. I coach multi-millionaires, some men and women who make tens of millions to hundreds of millions. They have, for the most part, most of their life, come from lack. Even though they have a bunch of money, they've come from a place of massive exhaustion because they've forced themselves all the way up the ladder financially in the business world coming from a place of fear and a desire to erase that fear.

Now, there's nothing wrong with the desire for something that's truly aligned with you, and that you're passionate about and, if it makes sense to your Kingdom work. But the problem with desire is that if it's something that's trying to fill a lack, scarcity and void, is that you'll end up with a view of life that's disappointing. As David will show you, you'll wind up with a false prosperity. In other words, if I keep getting things, but it's never filling my cup, then I'm going to think that this life is disappointing.

Now, do you think God wants you to live a disappointing life?

No, he wants you in creation. He wants you to be hopeful for the future. He wants you to be in faith that there is more, even when times are tough. Because in tough times, people without God can possess courage, and I think courage is great, but the problem with relying on courage all the time is that we're still coming from scarcity and lack if we're thinking we always need to be courageous all the time to be able to get somewhere.

When we move into acceptance, forgiveness, understanding, joy, love, peace, contentment, these are all the things that God's constantly calling us to, "come into this place," Jesus says, "I am the way, the truth, and the life." He knows how to transcend the matrix of the dark fallen kingdom, the structures of this world that are in place that constantly bombard us and suppress us to stay in the lower brackets of shame, guilt, apathy, and fear.

I believe in the Kingdom definition of prosperity that David is about to unfold in this book. I believe that we're co-creating with God, and we can lose our salvation. That's how important it is to understand that we have our Free Will, and we get to choose to be in that with Christ. In believing that we co-create with God, and God gives us our Free Will, I believe that He also gives us the ability to learn to trust ourselves and to trust him.

As a Christian that's committed to the Kingdom, I naturally want to invite Christ into my life to co-create with me. Imagine what a powerful experience to have him there with you. You trusting Him and you learning how to trust yourself in the way that He's designed you for. Imagine then what He has in store for you. But that's also saying there's more responsibility there, the more that is given to you.

I think that in walking with Christ there are blessings and times when he reminds us of what's really important. This is one of those times. Again, there is more to prosperity than wealth and I think there are so many of the structures in this world that take us away from that, that attempt to take us away from a true prosperity as was intended in the Bible.

The best part is that it's available to all of us. My point is that no one is ever too dirty to not have a shower. No matter how dirty you are, you stand under that shower and you are getting some of it off. It's washing off! I think that some people are so in their shame, their guilt and their sin and to them I say, "God doesn't want us in that."

The enemy of our soul wants us to doubt. The enemy of our soul wants us to feel like we're not worthy. The enemy of our soul wants us to feel that God doesn't have these incredible things in store for us and that he wants us in depression. He wants us to be useless. God wants to work with us. God wants us to move in a Kingdom fashion.

The enemy of our soul wants us to feel useless.

So in the pages that follow, I would pray that you are exposed to a progressive moving forward in hope. That you are not in your past, but that you are able to use the lessons and the resources that you've gleaned from it, and that you look upon tomorrow as a new day.

When you realize that what you can achieve in the future is far, far greater than what you've already achieved today, that's prosperity to me. We are really only scratching the tip of the iceberg with our potential. God has given us so much more.

CHAPTER 1

MY WAYWARD SON

Let no one in any way deceive you,
for it will not come unless the apostasy comes first
2 Thessalonians 2:3

We live in a rather crazy time, don't we? Sometimes you just have to take a moment and look at it from the outside to realize how bizarre we've made it. For instance, I feed my children chicken nuggets made from plants and shaped like dinosaurs. It's an interesting conundrum that doesn't make much sense but it's rather trivial in terms of the bigger riddles we've been asked to buy into. For instance, people always say they have no time, energy, or money, yet are more than willing to wait 30 minutes in a drive-thru for overpriced coffee filled with artificial sweeteners, which eventually causes their energy to crash even harder, winding up in the same place.

For instance, everything from the earth, we now refer to as "alternative medicine," yet "mainstream medicine" is largely created in a laboratory with synthetic materials.

There are millions of people walking the planet desperately seeking true love, but our culture is prone to binge-watch shows like *The Bachelor*, *Wife Swap* and *Keeping Up With The Kardashians*.

Every politician campaigns on balancing the budget yet the figures show from 2000 to 2019 the Federal Debt Increased 297 percent.

Nobody wants to be a victim of violent crime but studies show that 61% of prime-time television shows contain violence. That number goes up to 69% for children's programming.

So, let's begin by agreeing that despite our best intentions, we often do things contrary to what makes the most sense or gets the best results, because the majority of the time we're taking our direction from a fairy tale world where the same mistakes are repeated over and over but the outcomes are somehow expected to be different.

The problem is that somewhere along the way we became detached from our foundation and lured into a false reality that has led us further and further from the truth. Not just simple truth, but God's eternal wisdom. This wasn't by accident, it's not just the plan of a few bad seeds that popped up, it's part of the great deception of the fallen angel.

This is the story of humanity's rebellion against God and His desire to restore it.

For I know the plans I have for you, declares the LORD,
plans for welfare and not for evil, to give you a future and a hope.
Jeremiah 29:11

Throughout the world, on a mass scale, we've witnessed a shift. People have been encouraged to stop thinking for themselves as the evolution of social media and political correctness created a tsunami of groupthink. It's an attempt to strip us of our identity, second guess our natural intuition and give credence to things that don't sit well with our spirit or pass the common sense test.

Not only did we start to do and agree to things that didn't make much sense, but most of the time we weren't even sure why. We got so caught up in the world and just started moving in a particular direction or paying attention to something because everybody else was moving that way or paying attention to it.

I'm doing this because my governor said to do it. I'm thinking this way because that is what everybody else thinks. I'm watching this because I was told I needed to. I believe it because the news said I should. I'm reading this because everybody else said to read it. I'm following these instructions because this person of influence said these instructions made everybody who followed them successful and happy.

We've been lured into a world of drive-thru wisdom and subsequently disappointed by the false expectations which resulted from embracing it. It's distorted our perception of what to value, who we are and what exactly is truth. This is why most people walking the planet today are not operating in a fraction of what God called them to be, because we became loyal followers of man rather than pursuers of God's word.

Isn't it interesting how *follower* has become a word that blossomed in our culture? It's defined by Merriam-Webster as *to accept as authority; to be or act in accordance with*. Remember that, as the term *authority* will be important to our conversation throughout this book. It also brings up an initial question we must answer; by whose authority are we acting in accordance with most these days, God's or man's? In my opinion, if there's a happiness gap right now, that's where it appears to be, it's in not recognizing the difference between the two. Perhaps it's why so many of us feel like we're living the movie *Groundhog Day*, waking up each morning expecting something different, only to hear, feel and see the same things - fear, worry, lack and division.

It seems the world has become quite enamored listening to human authority over what God says, and that the world is acting in accordance with what man says now versus what God said in the beginning. This is nothing new in terms of ancient history, a history that repeats itself. Again, this is the story of humanity's rebellion against God and His desire to restore it.

Beware of false prophets, who come to you in
sheep's clothing, but inwardly they are ravenous wolves.
You will know them by their fruits
Matthew 7:15-16

Have you taken an audit of the world lately? Is man's wisdom producing more fruit or greater instability? That's a rhetorical question as anyone can see we're in trouble. When we, as humans, feel uncertain or unstable, we tend to panic and turn to God for answers. We light the signal fires and furiously wave our hands while looking up to the sky because we need help and we need it now. What we're seeing is an awakening of the spirit as people have begun to realize that maybe we can't do it without Him.

Not only do we need divine intervention with the big worldly problems like viruses, war, terrorism, tyranny and violence, but with our everyday personal struggles that still go on at the same time. Things like *how am I going to hold this marriage together, how will I ever get this business profitable, where will we find the money to pay the mortgage or send the children to school.*

It all adds up to stress, not success. Panic rather than prosperity. That is not how God planned it. We were created for more.

INFORMATION OVERLOAD

More, let's think about that word, shall we? In our quest to know more, achieve more and have more, it seemed like a good idea to consume more. That must be the solution in our quest for success and happiness, more. But wait, experts say the average person receives around 3.6 million gigabytes of information a day, little of which our mind has a chance to process among the 50,000 or so thoughts the average person has per day. Yet we continue to be in consumption mode, rarely slowing down or giving much thought as to what we're taking in or why? I compare it to taking my children into a yogurt store and telling them to be reasonable about the toppings, but they just can't seem to help themselves and end up with a heaping pile of things that don't go well together, which end up giving them an upset stomach. Information overload is the adult version of those toppings. In our quest to find happiness, we just keep piling on one thing after another, not stopping to think if it'll go well together or if it's going to make us sick spiritually.

And sick we are. You've heard about the thief who comes to steal, kill and destroy, yes? Information overwhelm appears to be a modern method of operation in the enemy's repertoire now. Whereas God is a God of order, peace and tranquility, what we're witnessing is the exact opposite of that, chaos, confusion and rage. The enemy knows that the more he can pour onto our plates, the more he can bombard our minds and disrupt our homes, marriages and communities with stress, the better means he has to divide us.

What I'm telling you isn't just a strong opinion but something I studied quite intensely while interviewing over one hundred corporate executives during the height of the 2020 pandemic. When questioned as to the greatest source of self-sabotage in their lives, by far the number one response given was overwhelm.

It's sadly ironic, isn't it, that in man's pursuit to make life easier we've only managed to complicate it and give ourselves over to greater confusion.

They say the future...it's on a microchip
Don't you know we're all on a sinking ship
Only ten percent control all the rest
Only ten percent decide what is best
(In Living Color - 1990)

Thirty years ago the group In Living Color sang those lyrics. The secret is not really a secret is it? We've known for quite some time where we were headed but sat idle, feeling as helpless bystanders. We as a country, a culture, a human race, now enter into this new season of our lives, one in which we find ourselves engaged in a new type of war, a war of information and misinformation. A war of deception and coercion. A war between the temporal inventions of man and God's eternal truth. Don't get me wrong, man's wisdom is certainly capable of providing valuable information, I don't argue that, but when it lacks foundation, when it's absent from its divine source and missing love, it's almost always dangerous.

FIX YOU

People all over the world are worried about their families and concerned about the future. Perhaps you're among the ones who, right about now, would like nothing more than to simply fix the world? But you know as well as I do that there are quick fixes and there are good fixes but there are very rarely any good, quick fixes.

This brings us to another part of the problem we face; we've been conditioned to want things fast and easy and that's rarely how success or happiness is achieved. So, first thing's first, we don't fix the world, we fix ourselves, and we accomplish that by slowing down to get ahead. Yes, it may seem counterintuitive to everything that our fast-paced culture has conditioned us to believe, but again, where have the fruits of that world gotten us?

Deciding exactly what we need to fix might seem obvious, but it's never that easy, is it? The fact is, we have so much information and so many choices that we have suffered a great deal in terms of our ability to focus and make confident decisions on what we want.

On the contrary, people have no problem vocalizing what they don't want.

On the personal side I often hear:

I don't want to be stagnant in life.

I don't want to make the wrong decision.

I don't want to constantly be seeking the counsel of others regarding what I should do.

I don't want to live with regret.

I don't want to be poor.

I don't want to wake up every day doing something I hate.

Most of all, I don't want to be in this same place at the same time again next year.

On a grand scale its:

I don't want to be locked down.

I don't want to be told what to put in my body.

I don't want to pay more taxes.

I don't want to have more of my freedoms stripped from me.

Most of all, I don't want to be in this same place at the same time again next year.

Do you know what all those answers point to? A fear-based mentality and you can't focus on fear and God at the same time just like you can't focus on what you don't want and what you do want simultaneously, because they compete for your attention. Why then do we seem to be so intent on focusing on fear? Because fear sells.

HIGHWAY
TO HELL

Although it feels like a sudden change, this strategy of overwhelm, distraction and confusion has been very cleverly and very subtly orchestrated over time. That's the way the enemy of our soul works best, by distracting us little by little, to the point where we get comfortable and put our lives on cruise control. You don't go from the greatest civilization the world has ever known, to one in fracture, overnight. As Christian author C.S. Lewis said, *"the safest road to hell is a gradual one."*

With that in mind, let me ask you, if you were to look around right now, could you pinpoint the exact spot you feel the world made a wrong turn? Probably not. You'd most likely think back to a time when you could recognize several things that seem quite obvious now but were rather inconsequential when they happened. Sure, you might have tilted your head to the side and thought something is not right about that, but it wasn't enough to make you put your foot down and demand clarity or correction. After all, we're so busy, who has time for that?

Again, this is not by accident, as Canadian psychologist Jordan Peterson pointed out in a 2020 interview when he said, *"Things get to terrible places one tiny step at a time. If I encroach upon you to the point where you protest, then I stop and I calm down and I wait, and then I keep doing that again and again in sequence, before you know it, you'll be back three miles from where you started. You'll say oh, how'd I get here. Well, I pushed you a little farther than you should've gone and then you agreed."*

You agreed, or *acted in accordance,* with an authority that went against your spirit. Maybe you were acutely aware of it, maybe not, but we did this both on a personal level as well as a whole, as a culture. We allowed ourselves to go on cruise control and accept little pushbacks, giving very little resistance because we trusted in man. And still, at this very moment, we're being asked to back up, little by little, and play by a different set of rules. Not only have we been asked to play by different rules, but we've been asked to believe the ingredients for a happy life have changed so drastically that we must be the only ones who feel like "Hey Dorothy, we're not in Kansas anymore." You've clicked your heels, but nothing is happening, nothing seems to have a sense of normalcy anymore. So, you wonder, maybe it's me, maybe I'm missing something?

Indeed, we are. We've misplaced the original instructions.

Do not forget my teaching,
but keep my commands in your heart,
for they will prolong your life many years
and bring you peace and prosperity.
- Proverbs 3

It doesn't get any clearer than that, does it? And please pay particular attention to that last word, *prosperity.* It's likely that your concept of what it means revolves around wealth and success and while that is certainly part of it, it only scratches the surface. If you're going to define prosperity by just that part, you're setting yourself up for disappointment.

What if I told you the biblical definition of prosperity means so much more than money? What if I told you that God's concept of prosperity will not only equip you to be more successful financially, but it will equip you to be a warrior of the spirit and triumph through whatever hardships this world throws at you.

Just wait, we'll get to it.

THE WAITING IS
THE HARDEST PART

How many times have you found yourself waiting and wishing for a sign, some type of permission to give you the green light that it's ok to be optimistic again? I know that we're tired of living in fear and we'd like nothing more than to go back to what was normal. It feels like a long time since we last felt normal, doesn't it? Did you know that there were nearly 400 years that passed between the last book of the Old Testament (Malachi) and the first book of the New Testament (Matthew)? During that time there were people who wondered where God had gone and many people lost faith. We're in a time such as that right now. Many people are questioning where God is when we need him the most, saying *God, we could really use you down here right about now. Things are getting out of hand.*

Time is one of the most prevalent themes of the Bible and something most of us struggle to reconcile with. It can be as tiny as why haven't I received a promotion at work or why haven't I had a productive date in months to the big struggles like when will the violence stop or when will the corruption go away. When we grow impatient, we ask God why He isn't doing something about this right now. It's a very normal thought because, for us living in the world, on earthly time, everything is urgent. We live in a culture where our internet speed and bandwidth can be purchased and upgraded in an instant so waiting on anything is something we don't like.

But isn't it funny how impatient we become waiting on God to go to work but when it's the other way around, when the shoe is on the other foot and God nudges us to move by taking action in our bodies (stop drinking), our marriages (talk it out) or direction of our business (take it to the next level), we're often slow to respond? Suddenly time isn't that critical of a factor.

Don't feel bad. God understands and gives us an opportunity to rectify the situation, and if a sense of urgency is exactly what you feel right now, it's a perfect time to catch up with both prayer and your actions.

Everything up to this point has been met with minimal resistance, perhaps because of human nature. It's like the man watching the forecast of a hurricane coming across the Atlantic for days on the news, but does nothing in hopes that it takes a sudden turn in another direction. Nine times out of ten, it does. This time the gamble didn't pay off, so it's either act or react. You now decide how to handle adversity, via man's advice or God's.

Many people will still look to earthly authority and ask *what does man say*? Isn't it obvious? Man suggests a "reset" because man doesn't want to admit his errors or mistakes and therefore asks for a do-over. Man also, and may I say rather ostentatiously, suggests we reimagine, another popular word used very often now. Yes, the earthy authorities would like us to reimagine realities that have been foundationally established by God. This is even more dangerous.

But what does God say? God says revival.

God doesn't need resetting or reimagining because His is *the way, the truth and the life* and so it simply calls for a revival. A revival is defined as *an instance of something becoming popular, active, or important again.* That something is the Word of God in our daily lives.

In the profound words of the spiritual mentor who inspired me to write this book:

We've been called to do something we don't have the means to accomplish. The size of the task (Noah) or physical state (Sarah) is always real. We can also look at our rejection (Samuel, David) and look at our delays (Moses) through the examples we were given in the Bible. Because there is nothing greater to do for your wholeness of life and the prosperity of your family than to submit to the wonderful, incomparable word of God.

I can't emphasize it any clearer than this. I'm in this spiritual war with you. These have been trying times for me and my family, so I know exactly how you're feeling. On a personal level, you've worried about what's next and stressing about an unknown future in an out-of-control world. *What's the plan,* you nervously ask your friends while having coffee. *What are we going to do* is the question that keeps popping up on the family text thread. We've all got big scary questions that we seek answers to, and I can tell you the typical responses:

(1) This problem is too big for little old me to do anything about.

(2) If we wait long enough, maybe it'll fix itself.

(3) Somebody's going to step up and lead us back.

No. No. And No. The answer is God has a plan and it involves you. It centers around the Body of Christ and it's super simple - *Get wisdom. Though it cost all you have, get understanding*

Let's not complicate it, we've turned away from truth, from God's wisdom, the instructions He gave us to live a fruitful and happy life. The world has been willfully disobedient and bowed to man's laws and man's instruction and now we're tasked with reviving the Word and bringing it back to every person who's willing to listen in order to redeem the world.

But again, we begin small. It starts with you and your understanding that God's book is all about the victory you hold in your hands. It was written for you and about you for times such as these. The author trumps all others, and the book is supernatural in nature. And so, at this juncture, it becomes my job to make the case that everything you desire in terms of success in life and peace in your heart is on the other side of the pursuit of the foundational wisdom of God's eternal truth.

DID YOU KNOW?

The Bible has more manuscript evidence than any other 10 pieces of classical literature combined.

Historians claim that there are more than 25,000 manuscript copies of the New Testament which have been identified, the oldest of which is thought to be no more than 125 years after the original.

Homer's Iliad is a distant second with somewhere around 1,500 manuscript copies, and with the oldest copy dated between 500 and 1,000 years after the original.

Homer's Iliad is what's most often compared to the Bible in terms of history and accuracy.

The Iliad contains about 15,600 lines of which 764 lines are in doubt. This means the Iliad manuscripts contain five percent textual corruption or uncertainty.

By contrast, the New Testament contains 20,000 lines with only 40 lines, or 400 words in doubt, which figures to 99.5 percent textual certainty, or only one-half of one percent of words containing variants (Giesler & Nix 366 367).

Any errors or inconsistencies found in the New Testament were in spelling or minor differences of style, none of which represent a challenge to any Christian doctrine or moral precept.

CHAPTER 2

SWEET LITTLE LIES

Do not heed the jar of man's warring opinions.
Let God be true and every man a liar. The Bible is the Bible still.
If any man lacks wisdom, let him ask of God
-Horatius Bonar

You may recall the famous exchange between Tom Cruise and Jack Nicholson in A Few Good Men, when Cruise's character slams his fist on the desk and passionately demands that he's given the truth. I think the situation in the world right now calls for that type of fiery exchange. We want answers, yes, but more importantly, we want the truth!

Suddenly we seem to live in a world unsure of the truth. There's this truth and that truth, their truth and our truth, and so we find ourselves in a watered-down assembly of half-truths, sold with the slickness of a serpent in all the places where foundational truth was most vulnerable to trickery; schools, entertainment, social media and government. Eventually, it even found its way into our churches.

How did this unraveling of truth happen? I think we can narrow it down to two things, we've either been led to look in the wrong direction for the right reasons or in the right direction for the wrong reasons. Let me say that again and slow it down. Somewhere along the way, we started looking in the wrong direction, meaning to the wrong people (actors, athletes, influencers and politicians) for the right reasons (how to steward money, how to have a successful relationship, how to raise a family, how to live healthy, how to not be afraid). In many cases, those wrong people convinced us to look to the wrong things (fame, wealth, vanity, violence, more government) for the right feeling (significance, love, self-worth, self-preservation, safety and security). In other words, we got a bunch of random advice from flawed and untested role models which produced a body of superficial results lacking any real substance.

The second part is a much tougher pill to swallow because the intention was better, however the results were the same. We looked in the right direction for the wrong reasons, meaning we knew we had to step into faith, to seek a higher authority, and so we looked to God (the right direction), but for the wrong reasons (instant gratification, the path of least resistance, notoriety, significance and wealth). We hit our knees praying for something the world was telling us was important because those same people mentioned above possessed such an influence over us and sold us on a false definition of happiness.

In other words, we prayed to an eternal, heavenly, God for temporary, superficial solutions and where did that get us?

Whether it was a faulty source or a false expectation, the outcome was the same; old feelings of lack and disappointment. So, we went back to the same old internal finger-pointing; What am I doing wrong? Why does happiness seem to elude me? Why can't I find a way to fulfill my dreams?

There you have it. The answer is right there, you failed because you had the wrong dream. You see, I'd been frustrated too, beating myself up in an attempt to conform to this world and what it says the definition of prosperity is. But then I heard those words whispered in my head over and over again saying, *David, you got suckered into chasing the wrong dream. You're chasing the world's dream, not God's plan for you.* I'd been seduced by a hollow definition of success and happiness because I fell into the trap of consistently listening to the advice of gods with a small g over that of God (big G). That's where I went astray.

OF GOD OR GODS

It seems we've done a very efficient job of creating gods (small g) out of men (and women) these days. They are quoted and praised on social media and cable news networks for their wisdom and accolades. This is really nothing new, man has always sought the guidance of teachers or experts. In ancient Greece, way before Wi-Fi, people looked to the advice of scholars who were exalted among gods, men like Pythagoras, Plato and Socrates. Individuals who were thought to have held the keys to all of life's questions as to how to acquire knowledge and success.

One such man was Aeschylus, known as the father of Greek tragedy. In regard to the search for prosperity, he said, **"It is easy when we are in prosperity to give advice to the afflicted."** In other words, when you're exalted among men because things are seemingly going well, it's easy to give direction to those struggling. And right now, there is no shortage of either, people who are struggling and those willing to give them advice on how to prosper.

My question is, if we have an abundance of great advice from gods (small g) then why aren't we witnessing an overabundance of happy and prosperous people walking around our neighborhoods or passing us by in the office or laying their heads down on the pillow next to us at home?

Again, where is the fruit?

To be clear, it isn't that the advice of these gods is always bad, it's that it often lacks foundation. It's not that we can't learn value from them, it's that there is typically a values inversion in them. To put it succinctly, the "strategies" are often before the Spirit, to a believer, the cart was before the horse as The Holy Spirit was not the filter of the advice. Again, does that mean the advice or strategy doesn't work or hold some value? No, not at all, but when my wife Angelike and I would try to implement worldly strategy in our business, it rarely aligned with the Word of God. In other words, there was often a great degree of direct contradiction. Great, we thought, so all those years, all that money and all that time, only to find out we'd missed this very important piece all along.

Be it an intentional deception or just a byproduct of our cultures desire to place profit over purpose, we, as believers, felt compromised. There was a growing discernment in our spirit which was telling us the Holy Spirit was not just being left out, but replaced.

YOU TELL ME THAT
IT'S EVOLUTION

One of the most deceptive little fabrications the gods of culture have attempted to sell us on is this notion that we're evolving and therefore in need of a completely new set of rules, which earthly authority just so happens to have. They say those old foundations, you know, based on scriptures in that old book, well, they're just outdated now and not as relevant in our advanced world. We're being told that we've become so technologically superior that we don't need the God of the Bible anymore, that we're "reimagining" what the God of our time should be like.

That is not how it works.

Some of the most powerful influencers of our time, in government, in entertainment and in social media, have been the ones who seek to "reimagine" God in a way that suits their lifestyle and their ideals. They have imagined this a-la-carte God who conveniently allows them to pick and choose which parts of the Bible are true and those which they deem are more malleable or flexible.

That is not how it works.

Then there are many whose thoughts are more along the lines of; look around at our progress and see what our human minds have come up with to make life better. We're so highly evolved, we can figure this out on our own without God.

I give you this warning, either is a dangerous place to plant your flag as scripture points out over and over again that when man goes astray and drifts from God's law, His instruction, it doesn't turn out good.

Again, definitions are important, so let's look at what it means to evolve; *to change or develop slowly, often into a better, more complex, or more advanced state.* This is the part in which I'd laugh if the stakes were not so high, but you get the news, you're on social media. We may be advanced and we're definitely more complex, but better? Really? Do you think so?

The body of results from this shift in worship from God to gods doesn't really present a great case for *better.* You have an entire generation renting, dating, job-hopping and Tweeting. It's not hard to see that we've been conditioned to go with what's easy and non-committal, which leaves people with a whole lotta "interests" but not a lot of "commitment" and without commitment, rarely does anything rich and meaningful get accomplished.

The modern and "evolving" concept of happiness resembles a pop-up tent, moving from place to place, trend to trend, like a gypsy, never setting up for long-term success or meaning. How can it though when the truth is constantly changing? We've been enlisted into this cat and mouse game in which we try so many methods and copy so many formulas that we forget where we started or worse, we lose sight of who've we've become along the way.

"I may walk slowly but I never walk backward."

Words spoken by the 16th President of the United States, Abraham Lincoln. They've been printed, studied, read and repeated in self-development books and seminars a thousand times when talking about how important perseverance is in life. And if there is one thing you need to know about Mr. Lincoln, there's no mistaking the source of his conviction or perspective. We know this, because written history tells us that upon receiving a Bible as a gift from a former slave in 1864, Lincoln responded writing:

"In regard to this great book, I have but to say, it is the best gift God has given to man. All the good the Savior gave to the world was communicated through this book. But for it we could not know right from wrong. All things most desirable for man's welfare, here and hereafter, are to be found portrayed in it."

Truer words were never spoken. Every one of us on this earth is waking up each day trying to better our lives as we desire deeper love, more wealth, better health and spiritual awakening. What Lincoln is saying here is that we've been given the ultimate instruction book, helping us not just to know right from wrong, but to point us toward all of those better things in life which we all desire.

Culture will tell you *we've evolved.* That's a lie. People haven't changed. Our country hasn't changed. It's the influence that has changed. And just as in Lincoln's time, our world is under a tremendous amount of pressure, but the one thing that holds true is that God has not changed. His desire has always been to restore our hearts. So, lest we forget, the God which Abraham Lincoln speaks of is also the God of Abraham, Isaac and Jacob, the one true eternal God. My point being that foundational wisdom is time-tested wisdom and although the world has changed, God's instructions and promises have not.

The beginning of wisdom is this, get wisdom. Though it cost
all you have, get understanding (Proverbs 4:7)

When you read this proverb for the first time you might've said but I'm trying to get wisdom. I'm taking all the courses and reading all the books. Sure, you know how to win friends and influence people. You've washed your face and told yourself you're a badass. You've read how to make your bed, shorten the workweek, 10 X your life and awaken a giant. You've gone left and gone right, listened to the fox and the peacock and yet you're still thirsting for meaning, you still feel incomplete in some way. The little gods haven't fixed your big problems because while they can help you pick out the window treatments and wall colors of life, they cannot lay the foundation.

Disappointment comes when we try to let them do that, when we put man in place of, or in front of, God. It's like the old saying, you're putting a Band-Aid on a bullet wound. What you got was a cultural education rather than foundational wisdom, more confusion than confidence.

Ecclesiastes tells us to use the Word of God like a guiding light and warns us to be cautious of man's attempts to add things or supersede the wisdom of Scripture… *of making many books there is no end, and much study wearies the body.*

I'd be foolish to say that the only book on your shelf should be the Bible. Not so at all. But it should be the first book on your shelf, the one which you measure all others by in order to judge their validity.

And for those who make the Bible their first book, its author should be your first teacher, and might I add the only author who will tell you that He loves you and means it.

Make sure you get that! That's a big *a-ha moment* when you realize that your teacher has a vested interest in your success because love is at the core of His message. That is what sets the Word of God apart from all others. It's based on an intimate relationship with you. When you look at the books on your shelf, how can you say that about any others? Have any of the other authors of those books professed to know you intimately or to love you with an everlasting love?

We should have a burning desire to learn but at the same time balance that with the discernment to seek teachers not simply based on trends or popularity, but foundational wisdom. I say this because I was guilty of it. I was under the assumption for a long time that more information was always good and that the spirit could always be separated from the speaker. However this was not true as my results moved me further and further from where I wanted to go. At certain points, I would literally have to leave discussion groups or exit a room because there was such a tremendous sense of darkness lurking in these so-called business philosophies.

"Teaching that is only knowledge and doesn't include love, what it results in, is thinking that information equals transformation. It's information in the context of a loving relationship that equals transformation."
- Pastor Mark Driscoll

In my eagerness to consume, consume, consume, I ignored any emphasis on compassion, authority and morality. What I learned was exactly what the above quote states, the teaching I was receiving was not a recipe for profound transformation in my life. It was just knowledge bereft of foundation. I discovered that when you add God, you add the spirit and the context with which to apply the knowledge and that is when you come into possession of a framework for radical and meaningful transformation.

And here's the crazy part, I know how much you'll pay for the wisdom of knowledge teachers, tens if not hundreds of thousands. Ironically, the wisdom in God's word you can find for free in the drawer of any hotel room across the country. So from a cost standpoint, it's a no-brainer, you have nothing to lose financially. From a spiritual perspective, the cost is much steeper.

I am now going to ask you, on a very personal basis, regardless of where you're at in your faith journey, what's holding you back from wanting to know more about the Word? And secondly, why do you think there are forces at work in this world that do not want you to read the Word or to obtain its wisdom? Why are some factions of the state and of higher learning so persistent about wanting to keep you in the dark?

A FAIRY TALE WORLD

God has been pursuing us from the beginning, from Genesis. He wants us, in our crazy, hectic and modern world, to know his story and how we fit into it. However, it would seem these days that people are more apt to put their faith in fairy tales than scripture. And when it comes to fairy tales, there are two characteristics that everyone possesses that are very relatable to what's happening in our culture right now; (1) somebody who has something versus somebody who doesn't and (2) somebody who seeks to know the truth versus another who seeks to hide the truth from them.

Whether it's beauty *(Snow White, Beauty and the Beast)* riches *(Rumplestiltskin, Jack and the Beanstalk)* or freedom *(Peter Pan, Rapunzel)* all fairy tales lead to where? Happily Ever After.

The Prince or Princess with the golden hair, the huge castle and the love of the people has personified guidance and hope for generations of young people. If we could only be like them and learn their lessons, then every day we too would wake up, pick up our mandolin and head to our garden singing songs in perfect pitch alongside the birds and other talking animals. That's typically how the fairytale goes, yes?

But what's missing? As legendary radio broadcaster Paul Harvey would say, "the rest of the story." Harvey was famous for always filling in the story behind the stories and that's important, because there's always more to a story than meets the eye. In the case of fairy tales it's what's known as the long journey home, meaning what happens after the princess is rescued or the spell is broken or the city is saved? We're rarely given a frame of reference to fill in those spaces. What we are left with is comparing how other's stories compare to our current reality.

Let me ask you this, what happens after you've listened to and done all that which culture says is important or coaches say delivers prosperity, yet you still feel something is missing? What does it feel like when your mentor hears your struggle and their only answer is "well, your problem is that your *why* isn't big enough."

You are a human being with real feelings and deep scars, and to look at life through a filtered lens of social media is unrealistic, but yet we've entered into rather strange times where a manufactured, or false, reality is enough for some people to call happiness. What we get are flattering versions of reality, kind of like fairy tales, where everything gets solved with a wish. Here's the formula, repeat it and voila, you're happy.

As members of the audience, the followers and consumers, we see this on our screen and assume the rest of the influencer's story is equally as amazing as their feed. Does she wake up looking that perfect? Wow, how does one keep a house spotless 24/7? Does that person ever eat a french fry? That couple must have sex every night. This is the world as it shows up via the screen on our phones and televisions.

Applying the first part of a typical fairy tale, they have something that we don't, so we think *that must be what I'm missing*. They're happy and here I am stuck in this house, talking to mice and washing the floors. It's the innocent and more understandable part of the fairy tale, a simple parallel of any culture, the desire to achieve something and overcoming the obstacles to get there. Not bad, but if you've been broken or have wounds that cut deep, waiting on a knight in shining armor or a Fairy Godmother isn't that great of a plan to rest your hopes on.

Now, let's examine the second part of every fairy tale, the more sinister part. That is where somebody (the villain) is holding something back from us. They are hiding some valuable piece of information or secret that would make our life much better. The most common example is the maiden or pauper who has no idea what talent they possess, how beautiful they are or that they are part of a royal bloodline.

The villain wants to keep this information from them because if they knew the truth, they would thwart their captor, escape their dungeon and break free from the spell they are under, thus queuing the happy ever after music.

The two big questions are, what truth is being held back from us and who benefits in keeping us from knowing it?

To answer the first part, let's look to the Psalmist David who wrote, *For you created my inmost being; you knit me together in my mother's womb. I praise you because I am fearfully and wonderfully made; your works are wonderful, I know that full well.*

David knew full well who made him, but do you? Trying to fathom the idea that we are knitted by God and we are known to him is hard for us to grasp. Of course we'd like to think that we were made for a purpose, that we are a masterpiece that matters but that thought is becoming increasingly harder for us to acknowledge because so much of our information and influence is coming from the world. We're so consumed looking outward for external fixes and solutions that we're missing the opportunity to look inward and hear what God says about us through our innervoice of discernment. I distinctly recall a preacher saying to me "the most underutilized power in the entire universe is that of the Holy Spirit."

Then why are we not tapping into that?

It's because of that second part, who wants to keep us from knowing such a potent and dynamic capability? Who benefits by keeping you in the dark? In fairy tale land, it's the villain and they typically cast a spell or give a potion, a literal concoction, that puts the hero or heroine to sleep or implies death so they will never find out.

In real life, villains don't wear black capes, have wretched faces or stand in front of a boiling cauldron. No, in our modern world they are much more cleverly disguised as C.S. Lewis so prophetically described in his Screwtape Letters saying that the: *"greatest evil is conceived and ordered in clean, carpeted, warmed and well-lighted offices, by quiet men with white collars and cut fingernails and smooth-shaven cheeks who do not need to raise their voices. Hence, naturally enough, my symbol for Hell is something like the bureaucracy of a police state or the office of a thoroughly nasty business concern."*

Interesting, isn't it? Quiet, clean shaven men with white collars. A police state run by a bureaucracy and big business. Lewis published that statement in 1942. He passed away in 1963. So, was he prophetic? Did he see something coming? Does this sound like anything you've witnessed happening in our world? Why would these men, this bureaucracy of government and big business, want you feeling insignificant and powerless? What is their benefit from you not possessing the power of the Holy Spirit?

More paramount, could they possibly trick you into unknowingly consuming poison?

Absolutely! While villains of children's fairy tales use the predictable potion, today's poison comes via messaging. Remember, this is a different war than in times past, this is a battle for your mind fought with words and ideas, two things which heavily dictate who has power and authority in our culture. Going back to God's word, he tells us this through King Solomon, who wrote in proverbs, *the tongue has the power of life and death.* The apostle James later confirmed those sentiments saying *the tongue is an unruly evil, full of deadly poison.*

I don't have to go into a long diatribe here, you've got a smartphone, the devil's playground is in your hand all day as we're under a constant bombardment of our thoughts. And who stands in front of microphones speaking with their unruly tongues most these days? Politicians, bureaucrats, big business, big tech, big pharma, big cable news, big entertainers and big influencers. They are the ones with the loudest voices and greatest influence in our society.

So, I'll ask again now, who benefits most from you not knowing you have power, from you not seeing your beauty and from you being unaware that you come from a royal bloodline? Many of those people I just mentioned. They control your language, your movement, your purchasing power and your thinking. All they ask in return is for your worship, your loyalty and your submissiveness.

PRESENCE AND INFLUENCE

It all comes down to this, who or what are you in the presence of most? In the secular self-development world you hear over and over again that you are the sum of the five people closest to you, a quote personal development guru Jim Rohn is most often attributed with saying. It is very true and there's nothing wrong with it, but how many people do you think choose their five based on worldly prosperity versus Godly principles?

How can one expect to wake up each day and be under the constant influence of culture, Monday through Saturday, and then expect to battle that, or even balance it out, by spending one hour in the Word on Sunday? The playing field is unbalanced and if you've had your eyes open, you know it's not an exaggeration to say that we're not only giving God less time but we're outright showcasing the enemy, making him the star of the show.

Think about it, every story you see on TV or social media concerning themes around pain, violence, racism, sex or greed only serves to promote the enemy and keep us in fear rather than faith. As I said in the first chapter, over 60% of prime-time programs contain violence. And what about the pandemic? What did the enemy do with the time that America was indoors on lockdown? He used it very wisely. His presence creeped into the televisions and devices of the people who stopped going outside and were most vulnerable to influence.

Consider this, the most streamed show of 2021 was *Criminal Minds*, a show about a Behavioral Analysis Unit of the F.B.I. which examines crimes of a serial and/or extremely violent nature. Viewers spent 33.87 billion minutes watching it in 2021 according to Neilson tracking. The top original series streamed was *Lucifer*, which received 18.35 billion minutes of viewing time. Not that the title leaves much room for doubt, but just in case you didn't know, it's a show about a handsome and powerful angel named Lucifer who leaves the depths of Hell to come to Los Angeles where he runs a nightclub called Lux.

In the words of Biff Tannen, "Hello, McFly. Is anybody home?" The new war of presence and influence is taking place right under our noses. We're welcoming it into our living rooms and bedrooms across the world. It's in the palm of our hand everywhere we go. We're outwardly saying we want peace, love and happiness but that's not what we're inviting into our homes or tuning into on our phones.

FIGHT THE POWER

I think the obvious question is, how do we fight this new war? People need to be reached and given the power of truth. But that truth is under assault and we're setting ourselves up for failure if we think we can win this spiritual battle only using God's word in ritual and recital for one hour on Sundays. Moses explained to us very clearly in Deuteronomy, it needs to be spoken about openly and often. We need to *impress it upon our children and talk about it when we sit at home and when we walk along the road. It needs to be written on our hearts and placed upon the doorframes of our houses.*

We war like the Apostle Paul told us to war, not with the weapons of the world but with the divine power of the Spirit. We demolish strongholds and arguments that set themselves up against the knowledge of God by spending more time discussing and teaching His word in the presence of friends and family. That's the first part. Then we win the battles on a daily basis, by bringing the lessons of scripture into our businesses and the city streets and on social media. Our greatest weapon is real talk about the real value found in real stories of the Old and New Testament. Because it's a relational word from a relational God, don't you think it should be discussed in a relational setting? Think back to high school or college. Were the classes you retained the most from those which the professor just lectured, or were they the classes that invited dialogue and interactive conversation? Of course we need Pastors, those well versed in doctrine, to guide the flock and impart the Word, but we really need to start participating in bringing the discussions out of the church and into the community, around the dinner tables, water coolers and parks.

It's time to take "The Church" out of its box because the world is broken and God is begging to reach the ears of those who've been lost in the wilderness, who've gone astray and gotten comfortable with culture. But just like with our own children, we can't say "believe, just because." We can't make or force people to believe, they have to be spoken to, heard from and then choose for themselves to accept the invitation. Remember, perhaps most important, we are told that as leaders who speak the Word of God , that others should be inclined to look at the outcome of our way of life and want to imitate our faith.

THE CHOICE IS YOURS

One very important point that cannot be overstated is that we are given free will. God uses encouragement, promptings and leanings of the Holy Spirit, but never coercion, never force, never control. He is not a micromanager. We, as individuals, either choose him or reject him based on free will. You get to decide which tongues touch your ears and what words and images you set before your eyes. The question you need to ask yourself is, will the foundation you build upon originate from a source that benefits your worshiping them rather than you worshiping your maker?

The prior may come at a cost, as we're told by the Apostle James that a friendship with the world often means a hostility toward God, and isn't that how this power shift, from God to gods has taken place? By gradually aligning ourselves with the concepts of cultural and worldly principles rather than scriptural ones. This is how we've canceled out the truth.

Right now, humanity has the perfect opportunity to course correct and seek truth. In order to convince people to make that decision, there's a simple question; whose plan do you think provides a better vision for the future, God's or man's? Who offers confidence over confusion, proof over empty promises? Where is there more fruit and opportunity?

That's what this is about after all, opportunity, a word that gets thrown around so often in our lives that it's almost like background noise to most people now. We hear it so much that we go right to our pessimistic and sarcastic internal voice which says *Yea, yea yea, I know, I know, you've got an opportunity for me, something that's gonna change my life. But let me guess, there's only a couple spots left and I'd be perfect for it.*

The *ACT NOW* messages which flood our inboxes or pop up on our screens are often swiped or deleted without second thought. Why? Because most of the time we know it's just somebody trying to get our money. They want to sell us on a product or program we don't need. But the stakes are higher when it comes to truth. That's something we desperately need. So think of God's sending you one more ACT NOW message of his own. In this day when everybody is fighting for your attention, there's God, still patient, still waiting to give you another opportunity to step into co-creation, to get closer to him. His offer is to free you from exhaustion, from frustration and turn your attention back to what works. Opt in for his course. It's got more testimonials and more proven results than all others out there combined.

LET'S GET A LITTLE BIT UNCOMFORTABLE

I end this second chapter in humility, telling you that I worked on this book for more than a year, and in the process went through heavy spiritual warfare. The enemy of my soul made me question my sentences, made me question how bold I would be, made me question who I would appease and who might I offend. This delayed my deadline and cost me many sleepless nights, even arguments with my family who begged to have their husband and father back. That's how much time I spent in front of a computer trying to figure out the perfect words to speak to you.

Eventually I had to take this book to the altar. I had to find a new obedience to God, meaning not just to listen, but to act on what I was hearing. In the Hebrew language there is a very specific and meaningful word for this, it's called Shema (sh'-mah). It means to hear God as in Deuteronomy 6:4 when we read *"Hear (shema) O Israel, The Lord our God, the Lord is one. You shall love the Lord your God with all your heart and with all your soul."* But it doesn't just mean to hear, it means to listen, comprehend and take action. That was my journey in writing this, listening first and in obedience, second, knowing that His words are better than my words, His strategy better than my strategy. And so, I asked what words were meant to be left out and what words meant to be left in, even as the writer in me wanted control and craved structure, I had to let God build these chapters. I had to let Him do his work in me. I had to let him build it.

What do you want to build? How strong do you want it to be? Will you shema, listen and act? Will you, as C.S. Lewis wrote, let him build?

"Imagine yourself as a living house and
God comes in to rebuild that house.

At first, perhaps, you can understand what He is doing. He is getting the drains right and stopping the leaks in the roof and so on; you knew that those jobs needed doing and so you are not surprised.

But presently He starts knocking the house about in a way that hurts abominably and does not seem to make any sense. What on earth is He up to?

The explanation is that He is building quite a different house from the one you thought of - throwing out - a new wing here, putting on an extra floor there, running up towers, making courtyards.

You thought you were being made into a decent little cottage: but He is building a palace. He intends to come and live in it Himself.

Let Him build

DID YOU KNOW?

That prior to 1993 there was no archeological evidence to collaborate the existence of King David? In July of 1993, at an ancient mound called Tel Dan, in Northern Israel, Archeologist Gila Cook found proof of King David's existence outside of the Bible when she uncovered a ninth-century B.C. stone (stela) with the Hebrew Words "House of David" and "King of Israel" on it.

Not only did this prove that King David was a genuine historical figure, but the stone, which originated from one of ancient Israel's fiercest enemies more than a century after David's death, still recognized David as the founder of the kingdom of Judah.

Why is King David so important to the Bible? He was a shepherd, a musician and giant slayer. He was an underdog, he was a sinner and most importantly, he was known as a man after God's heart, the only person referred to this way in the Bible.

David demonstrated courage, sorrow, repentance, humility, compassion and love. The Word also stated that the Messiah would come from the House of David.

Therefore when archeology found proof of the House of David in the Tel Dan stone, it was extremely significant.

CHAPTER 3

BREAKING THE MATRIX

If whatever men know comes through their brain without the Holy Spirit regenerating their spirit, then their knowledge will help them not one whit. If their belief rests in man's wisdom and not in God's power, they are merely excited in their soul.

-Watchman Nee

Some mornings it takes everything we have just to get out of bed and gather the energy to make a contribution to the people living in our own house, let alone the world. So, I know when you hear that the Holy Spirit dwells within you and is building a new house, it can be a pretty heavy concept to wrap your head around.

You might say that sounds great, but I certainly don't feel like one of God's creations. I agree. Of course, you're not feeling like the temple of God dwells in you because the modern world has done such an efficient job of stripping us of any connection with his other marvelous creations.

If you look at an aerial photo of the places with the largest concentrations of human beings, that being big cities, it's easy to see these are also the places most devoid of anything that resembles God's original design for us.

And the Lord God planted a garden eastward in Eden;
and there he put the man whom he had formed. (Genesis 2:8)

I know it's not practical to say we could live outdoors, in gardens, but what man has created as a sanctuary is in fact just a concrete jungle with eggshell colored walls and artificial lights. Like Joni Mitchell once sang, *we paved paradise and put up a parking lot.* So can we blame people when they throw up their hands in frustration because they are having a hard time connecting with God.

In his book Unfriended, author Joe Battaglia writes, ***"If we strip away the things of nature that, by design, communicate a sense of order, tranquility and transcendence, then society will gravitate toward the antithesis of those things - disorder, stress and focus of the self."***

It's easy to point the blame at Covid for hating lockdowns, but the fact is we, as a culture, began construction on our own personal prisons way before that. We've willingly surrendered such a large part of our daily existence to being immersed in things that are so far removed from God and his creation that we can't see how much of our creativity, our life force and our freedom has been stripped from us.

Sure, we have momentary glimpses of clarity and the occasional feeling as if God might be conspiring to do something in our favor but in general, we're relying on four walls and a small screen in front of our face to give us a large view of the majesty we call earth.

Go to Genesis and read how God created paradise and how He clearly describes it as being "good." He said the waters were *good*, the green plants were *good*, the sun and the stars were *good*, the creatures of the sea, winged birds, livestock and wild animals were all *good*. Just because you drink water, eat vegetables and go to sleep when the sun goes down doesn't mean you're in tune with God's creation. Things change on a spiritual level when your feet touch the ocean, when you listen closely to the rustle of the trees, when you see a thousand stars in the night sky and when you ride the back of a horse.

Maybe you can't go to the beach every day or live on a ranch, but when you begin to make it a daily priority to find one little piece of God to connect with, something outside of your home, in nature, that speaks to creation, then your spirit will intuitively seek a greater connection with God.

SLOW DOWN – YOU MOVE TOO FAST

Did you know that the average person spends 25 minutes each day at the kitchen sink? This equates to more than six days spent washing dishes each year. Research also shows the average adult in the United States spends more than 6,259 hours a year glued to the screens of phones, laptops and televisions.

Now consider this: The average American spends a total of three minutes a day in prayer. That means we spend eight times as much time tending to dishes as we do our spirit. Moses told the Israelites "the Lord will fight for you, you need only be still." Psalm 46:10 says *be still and know that I am God.*

It's no secret that presence counts, and that's hard these days when we have difficulty focusing our attention on anything peaceful and quiet. Time spent in tranquility and prayer is a direct lifeline to Him. If you are what's called a squirrel, like me, it's extremely hard sometimes to find that peace to speak intimately with God. If you're like me, you literally have to force yourself to slow down and create an environment where you can't be lured by distraction or by a ping of a device. And if you're anything like me, I'd be willing to bet that at some point you were told by your spouse or a loved one that you needed to slow down and be present more with the ones who love you. You quite possibly even made a promise to spend less time on your phone or computer and more quality time with them.

How did that work out?

One of the funniest things about human nature is that we have no problem in knowing what's good for us, it's in actually doing it that we find difficulty. When it comes to spending quality time in the presence of God or family, we know it feeds our spirit, but we can't shake the allure of these devices.

Know this, it's not entirely your fault. It's by design. The beeps and buzzes of push notifications combined with the flickering lights and high-definition images all create a sensory stew of sorts, geared toward intentionally hooking us, the user, into an addiction not much different from that of drugs.

Research shows that reacting to the lights and sounds of our gadgets, playing video games or checking status updates, releases the feel-good neurotransmitter dopamine in similar amounts to what might be found in people who have taken stimulants such as amphetamine or methylphenidate.

This need for constant stimulation is why people immediately pull out their cell phones when they're waiting in line at the coffee shop or at the doctor's office or at the airport. Technology has created a significant wedge in human interaction and in our ability to overcome the overwhelm and just be still.

WHO'S ZOOMIN' WHO

Authority and influence are the real commodities of the 21st century. It's why companies will pay for your contact list and why cookies always pop up asking to track you. I'm not asking you to throw away your phone and live off the grid, but are your devices taking dominion over you and, if so, to what degree are you willing to combat them and fight back?

To be fair and realistic, technology is not bad. It has no consciousness or nature, therefore it is indifferent. So, when people ask, is the Devil *in* a smartphone? No, but can he *reach people* through one? Yes. However, the same can be said about God. Is God *in* a smartphone? No. Can He *reach people* via one? Absolutely.

We can't demonize the actual technology, but we can look at who is behind it and how they manipulate it through deception on an unsuspecting public. When I say unsuspecting, maybe I should say confused. We're confused as a culture because we've been overwhelmed with information and completely missed the concept of what it means to be free. Let me ask you this, in the beginning of The Matrix, before Neo was contacted by Morpheus, did he think he was free or in a form of enslavement? He thought he was free right? He was so entrenched in technology, he became unaware of the boundaries between it and reality.

The Matrix is just a modern version of many biblical stories surrounding coercion and deception. Diversion and manipulation have always been mechanisms to draw God's people away from His presence and his laws. And while we don't want to go into a panic every time we turn on the television or our phone, we must be on alert.

Peter warns us to *be sober-minded and watchful because our adversary, the devil, prowls around like a roaring lion, seeking someone to devour.* Charles Spurgeon says *"the most poisonous serpents are found where the sweetest flowers grow."* I tell you, with the utmost confidence, that you need to be on alert as deception, particularly in the form of words and video showing up on our devices, will pose as one of the greatest threats to humanity over the next decade and beyond. The eyes which we've always trusted to see the truth, and the ears, with which we've always relied on for listening for the truth, will deceive the best of us. Neo was caught up in disbelief because what he was seeing and hearing were his reality, only it wasn't. It was a deception.

A WORLD OF INFLUENCE IN THE PALM OF YOUR HAND

Set aside the sinister thoughts of being unwillingly programmed or subliminally messaged by a device and just ask yourself this, would you agree that constantly looking at social media and the news on our devices contributes to a distorted worldview?

These devices have changed the way we work and communicate, often contributing a great deal to our success. But, the more we scroll on these devices simply because we're bored, the more we subject our minds to things that really don't concern us, things that we don't need to see nor bother ourselves with and the more we are distracted from the things, right under our noses, in our own house that we are neglecting or missing.

Genesis 3:1 says *in the garden the serpent was more subtle than any beast God had made.* It would be almost impossible to convince a stable person to willingly neglect their loved ones, but on the gradual road which Lewis spoke of, this mental slavery of media and devices let's call it, is that subtle serpent. To use a popular term, we humans are *trending* toward becoming simple facsimiles of what we were really created for.

But you could never be Neo you say, that's just science fiction. Or is it?

Not according to one of the smartest and wealthiest men alive, Elon Musk. During a 2021 interview on the Joe Rogan Podcast, Musk said *"Most people don't even realize, they are already a cyborg. That phone is an extension of yourself."* He said there is a tiny connection between our biological self and our digital self that will go from a straw-like flow to a raging river in the not-too-distant future. He then said "*if your biological self dies, you can upload it into a new unit... literally.*"

Rogan's reply was "pass the whisky."

Yea, I agree Joe, that comment got my attention too. And while I can't say what the average person thinks of a statement like that, I feel I can speak for the Body of Christ in saying, it's clearly in violation of anything God has told us in Scripture.

The deception has begun, and it's subtle, disguising itself as cute and harmless at first. It's an innocent little app that turns your face into a cartoon and auto-tunes your voice. You make them with your children and send them to your friends and everybody laughs.

But I want you to think about apps like Snapchat, Reface and Face Swap and how they've made their way into our lives with the innocence of a child. Think about how our eyes and ears are so critical to our discernment and therefore so susceptible to betrayal. So when a friend sends you a funny video of somebody face swapping Tom Cruise or President Trump, we laugh. It's always through the slight opening in the door, in this case, comedy or entertainment, that the devil enters. Deception is his weapon and if we can't see truth and decipher real from fake, where does that put us? In a tough spot.

They exchanged the truth about God for a lie,
and worshiped and served created things rather than the Creator
Romans 1:25

Whether you realize it or not, you've already begun the process of giving yourself over to a counterfeit, or digital, version of yourself by giving up your God given voice and image.

It's an enticing seduction. Everybody wants to be more beautiful or more knowledgeable. Eve certainly did. And now everybody wants to be the first to purchase land in the new frontier, an alternate reality. It's innocent after all, simply a form of role playing or an alternate way of doing business.

But is it innocent?

People say the Metaverse is brand new, but the idea is not. Do you remember shows like Fantasy Island and Westworld? These were places where men and women could go and do things they fantasized about but couldn't have in the real world. When it was over the people returned to their normal lives back home without repercussions. But look at the storylines, they were written by man and revolve around plots that were immoral most of the time. The allure of going to another reality for pleasure or vanity in a world devoid of God, his laws or accountability was their hook. So, the idea has always been in man's head, but now technology has caught up with the means for man to do it.

What begins innocently, with what God creates (earth), Satan corrupts (virtual earth). Imagine a place where twisted fantasies of rape or murder now go beyond gaming and the two dimensional world. Is crime even a thing in this fictitious world? We're moving at a pace so fast that we don't have time to look at or consider the consequences. There are a lot of things man is embracing about science before we can tell the ramifications for certain. What is certain is that scripture says *the thoughts of the wicked are an abomination to the Lord*. Not the actions, but the thoughts. God will bring everything, every secret deed, into judgment. *But Jesus, knowing their thoughts, said, "Why do you think evil in your hearts?* (Matthew 9:4)

> *Just as Eve was deceived by the serpent's cunning,*
> *your minds may somehow be led astray from your sincere*
> *and pure devotion to Christ.*
> *2 Corinthians 11:3*

Ask yourself these two questions, where are our eyes and attention most often these days and then, where is deception most likely to occur?

Don't you find it even the slightest bit ironic that a once bitten apple is the logo on the device which most of us use to obtain knowledge from the gods and idols of our era? As of January 2021, there were 1.65 billion Apple devices in use across the globe and a CNBC All-America Economic Survey reports the average American household owns 2.6 Apple products.

Jean-Louis Gassee, a Former Apple executive who worked there from 1981-1990 said, *"One of the deep mysteries to me is our logo, the symbol of lust and knowledge, bitten into, all crossed with the colors of the rainbow in the wrong order. You couldn't dream of a more appropriate logo: lust, knowledge, hope and anarchy."*

I can't argue with him. What's a more recognizable symbol of lust and knowledge than a once-bitten apple? It's almost too obvious. While I won't go so far to say that Apple was created for destructive or malevolent purposes, even a skeptic would have to admit that it's intriguing to ask what type of influence and dominion it has in our homes. As one researcher said *"I cannot think of any other product that has that kind of permeation with the public and level of growth."*

Here is what I find fascinating. Apple co-founder Ronald Wayne had a very different marketing idea. His initial logo was of Issac Newton sitting under a tree with an apple simply hanging over his head. The caption read *"Newton... A Mind Forever Voyaging Through Strange Seas of Thought ... Alone."*

Isn't that interesting and prophetic that the word *alone* was present in the original Apple slogan. Has there ever been a time that you wondered where your spouse or child was and after looking all over the house you found them sitting with their device....alone, sometimes for hours on end. Have you ever seen four teenagers at a food court all sitting at a table together but almost oblivious to one another, each alone in their devices. I call it the Great Separation, one from both other human beings and reality.

You may also find it interesting that in *Dante's Inferno*, the Italian poet places Satan frozen in ice at the center, or ninth circle, of Hell. This image is often interpreted as Satan being so far removed or separated from God's love, God's warmth, that he is frozen. Some Christian scholars argue that hell is not the fire and brimstone often spoken about by preachers but rather a separation from God and his love. Whichever you might believe, isolation is never good for the human spirit, it's why prisoners are held in solitary confinement. It breaks their spirit.

This brings us to connection and community, two of the other popular words of our culture. When do we get most frustrated these days? How about when we have a bad or slow connection to the internet. When it's down, people go into fits. It's equally laughable and disheartening.

Survey your friends on whether they'd be more willing to go a day without the internet or a day without seeing their spouse and I bet you get some frightening answers.

We've been lulled into a false sense of connection, believing that virtual connection is the same as a physical one. Perhaps you've heard people say *I've built an online community.* Okay, but if it's entirely online, then it lacks one of the most critical components of community, that being proximity.

Didn't we find out how much proximity meant to us during the pandemic and the lockdowns? Sure, Facetime helped us stay in touch with friends and relatives and Zoom helped us to conduct our business but look at the repercussions, we're now finding out the high cost of isolation as depression, addiction and suicide skyrocketed when we were forced to conduct all of our relationships in the virtual world, yet here we are poised to embrace the next level of disconnection.

ONE IS THE
LONELIEST NUMBER

According to the US Board of Labor Statistics, in 2020, people living by themselves spent an average of 11.3 hours per day completely alone. Alone with God is a good thing, alone in our head without him can be a scary place. How many times during the height of lockdowns do you recall the news warning of the dangers of isolation? Hardly ever. It was always looked upon as an unspoken consequence but never a priority. However, a person alone is often a spirit broken and God clearly points this out on several occasions in scripture.

The LORD God said, "It is not good for man to be alone.
(Genesis 2:18)

Paul warns the Hebrews to not give up meeting together.
(Hebrews 10:24-25)

One who has isolated himself seeks his own desires;
he rejects all sound judgment. (Proverbs 18:1)

Two people are better off than one,
for they can help each other succeed.
(Ecclesiastes 4:9-10)

A person standing alone can be attacked and defeated,
but two can stand back-to-back and conquer.

Three are even better, for a triple-braided cord is not easily broken.
(Ecclesiastes 4:12)

It's not a difficult debate to win. It's clear we were made to be in community together, in close proximity with one another as well as our creator. That's wisdom based in foundational truth. But if you've never seen those scriptures, how would we be sure that the authority of God supersedes that of man?

Let's go back to Apple and the man most associated with it, Steve Jobs. He said in his biography that he had a 50-50 belief in God and really only started to think about faith more after he got cancer. It's a sad but very common reality for people to only think about God when circumstances are dire and as a last minute plea for help.

Isaac Newton, on the other hand, was a physicist, an inventor and a believer. In fact, Newton studied the Word of God so diligently that he attempted to extract specific scientific information from scripture, even trying to predict when the world would end, which he said would come no later than 2060.

Of his many recorded thoughts, the one I find most interesting as it relates to the concept of authority I've been discussing, is this:

This most beautiful system of the sun, planets, and comets, could only proceed from the counsel and dominion of an intelligent Being. This Being governs all things, not as the soul of the world, but as Lord over all; and on account of his dominion he is wont to be called "Lord God"

There is that word dominion again, defined as *supreme authority, ownership, control or the power to rule.* As the digital age progresses, there will continue to be a war for our attention, and with our attention comes our thoughts and I don't hesitate to say that with our thoughts, go our souls.

Giving dominion over your life, be it willingly or unintentionally, comes with a price. I don't have to provide a statistic for that because you have eyes to see. You saw earthly authority with *rules for thee but not for me.* Every day you're witness to people at airports, at coffee shops, or just walking down the street, and where are their heads looking? Down. Looking down to find significance, looking down to find direction, looking down to find happiness.

Is that where you want to be, a clone in the matrix, or will you finally see the deception and be a rebel to culture who looks up for significance, looks up for direction and looks up for happiness?

DID YOU KNOW?

The Dead Sea Scrolls were one of the greatest archaeological discoveries of the 20th century. Discovered accidentally in 1946 near Palestine by teenage boys tending their herds of goats, the papyrus scrolls were hidden inside large clay jars.

The Isaiah Scroll was found almost entirely intact (all 66 chapters) and was one thousand years older than any fragment which had previously been discovered.

Carbon dating on some fragments suggested that they were from somewhere between 1,900 and 2,400 years old.

In the 70 years since these ancient documents were found in the Qumran caves, scholars have meticulously assembled thousands of fragments into more than 900 scrolls.

CHAPTER 4

REBEL REBEL

The Christian is a holy rebel loose in the world
with access to the throne of God."
- A. W. Tozer

Try to remember back to your teenage years when we begin to establish our identity, develop values and test authority for the first time. I was a rather rebellious teen when it came to taking orders. The answer "just because" never sat well with me and so I questioned a lot, always needing more clarity as to why. If you're a parent now, like me, it's probably one of the things that frustrates you most about your own children, but it's not such a bad thing. In fact, I'd argue that you should praise it, perhaps silently, as it will serve your children well when they get older. To blindly follow anybody or anything when the reason is "just because" is quite dangerous.

Unfortunately, there's a huge price to pay now when it comes to questioning the status quo or group think. It's this clever new weapon of the enemy called cancellation, which is a significant tool used by cultural keyboard warriors and many authority figures in an attempt to render the authority of God's foundational wisdom mute. In a "cancel culture" it's agree or else. Or else what? Or else you risk public castigation on social media by being labeled a bigot or having your livelihood threatened. Any tool which strips somebody of their individuality and coerces them into a place where they are too frightened to stand up for their beliefs out of fear of isolation is dangerous.

I've heard good people of strong faith say *just to play it safe, maybe you better not say it or post it.* A word of caution, playing it safe or claiming ignorance will not be an excuse come judgment day as we are clearly warned by God to be careful of such choices, especially when they contradict his word. Proverbs 24:12 says *if you say "But we knew nothing about this," does not he who weighs the heart perceive it? Does not he who guards your life know it?"*

Cancel culture has become a test of authority: will you bow to God or will you bow to man? People are afraid to make that decision, so they try to play it in the middle where it's safe and there's no right or wrong, no harm, no foul. But the lukewarm fence is a dangerous one to straddle because if you try to stand for everything, you stand for nothing and that does nothing to serve you, your family or God.

Navigating the line between what God says and man says is difficult. Ephesians guides us to the answer when it says take the helmet of salvation and the sword of the spirit. Helmets are worn for protection and the sword of the spirit is not a physical weapon but the infallible word of God. It's a very clear message, not of intolerance or violence, but one which describes courage and righteousness as standing up for foundational truth.

"I have given them thy word; and the world hath hated them,
because they are not of the world, even as I am not of the world"
John 17:14

There is a loving rebellion of the world that comes with being a disciple of Christ. There will be a time when you, the believer, are in stark contrast to what the world and its distractions say. You'll have to be firm in some things, which will not be popular. It doesn't mean we can't love people, we just don't have to be in agreement with what they say.

This speaks directly to the thoughts of A.W. Tozer who I began this chapter with. He said, ***"I believe you can be right with God and still not like the way some people behave. Our admonition is to love them in a larger and more comprehensive way because we are all one in Jesus Christ, this kind of love is indeed a Christian virtue."***

GET UP STAND UP

In the pursuit of wisdom and righteousness, we have to look to *Proverbs 4* to get clarity, as it says get wisdom at any cost. English minister Matthew Henry interpreted the proverb like this; *wise and godly men, in every age of the world, and rank in society, agree that true wisdom consists in obedience, and is united to happiness.* He said to *take pains for it so that it may rule over corruption.* In these times, we fight corruption at every level of government, from the school board all the way to the White House. True wisdom of scripture is the guide that never fails, the measuring stick that supersedes all that we will encounter. It's our obedience in fixing ourselves that leads to happiness. To take *pains for it* means it's not the easiest choice. It is the road less traveled. But in the end what happens? It puts an end to corruption.

That is why there are those who are trying to bury the Word or twist what it says. They are betting on the wrong side of history. If we are to take up the helmet and the sword, it means being able to weather criticism from culture and rejection from the world. It means to stand up to school boards who are trying to indoctrinate our children. It means getting off of cruise control in our communities and not allowing the mistakes of those who rule this world to continue to go unchecked.

The concept of being a *Holy Rebel*, or loving as Jesus would, is influenced much differently today than it would have been when Jesus walked the earth, or even in the mid 20th century when Tozer did. Why? Because we live in a world heavily persuaded or shaped by media and pop culture influence. We see and hear everything, so we aren't just presenting to a handful of people on a hillside somewhere, but rather to the world with the push of a button. This brings about a great dilemma; how do we present ourselves as followers of Christ in a time as volatile as this and still battle with forces who have no ethical measuring stick and don't play by the rules?

On one side, you have those who take the image of Jesus flipping over tables in the Temple as license to gravitate toward physical aggression, as if the Son of God would come into town with a nine-millimeter in each hand yelling F-bombs at anyone who challenges conservative morality.

Not likely. Yes, Jesus flipped over tables, but he wept, healed the sick and washed the feet of his disciples. He was both a lion and a lamb. He used wisdom, which Proverbs 4 just told us to get, in order to subdue his enemies.

But then you have the antithesis of that, the uber pleasant and politically correct Ned Flanders of The Simpsons, a believer who walks around in a cardigan and turtleneck saying howdy neighbor as he becomes a punching bag for ridicule.

What's called for is something somewhere in the middle of both these extremes.

I've needed a lot of pruning in my walk because I gravitated toward the first example. I leaned toward being an aggressive table flipper and still am to some degree, but Angelike has done a great deal of work helping to point me toward the bold, yet compassionate character of Christ. Time after time she's reminded me of scripture, which says the wood of the cross is way more powerful than the wood of the bat, metaphorically speaking of course. Meaning nobody wants to be beat over the head with a Bible and that we must lead by example. We must stand with the authority and compassion of God as if He is by our side at every step.

This is where I see Tozer's words so clearly. You can be right with God and still not like the way some people act. The asterisk or addendum being to repent first and be humble, accepting that we're all imperfect. But at the same time, there is a clear biblical distinction between being ignorant of God's Word because you've never been exposed to it and being willfully ignorant, meaning you see it and understand it, but choose to not accept it because it's not convenient to your business practices or lifestyle choices.

That being said, there is a sifting, or purification, happening amongst us, a grand refining of humanity between those who will choose to be bold in their convictions and put their name on the line when they see something misaligned with the will of God and those who choose to bow to culture and place their identity in the world. Those who stand up for God's word will be called rebels and their devotion to His truth will appear as a defiance to culture, but so be it, as victory does not come without risk. In the words of the great reformist Martin Luther,

"If you preach the gospel in all aspects with the exception of the issues which deal specifically with your time, you are not preaching the gospel at all."

There is a particularly intense fight happening right now, one which, as Luther says, we must preach about in our time. I'm speaking about the war on the nuclear family, the foundational institution, ordained by God, who commissioned man and woman to be fruitful and multiply. (Genesis 1:28). Procreation is a miracle which God blessed humanity with and He designed it for a husband and wife, biologically. Follow the science as we've been told. I've mentioned earlier that we're being asked to believe truths that go against God's truth and this is one of the biggest.

Culture has made it a sin in its eyes to state this fact publicly by injecting political correctness into this most contentious issue of our time, and sadly, the enemy has verbally handcuffed a bulk of the Church as well.

For out of fear, nobody spoke openly.
John 3:17

Fear, the preferred instrument of coercion throughout history, shows up, not as it did in ancient times, with scourging and death, but in this new war of canceling and forced isolation. It's perpetuated on nearly every TV channel, every social media platform and every level of public service. Say nothing, do not challenge anyone, you must take no stance other than that which culture takes or else. We've been told in a not-so-subtle way to fall in line with earthly authority and keep your fundamental Christianity for church on Sundays.

So out of fear nobody spoke, and the Word got pushed back. And they (culture) encroached a little more, and the Word got pushed back. They pushed again a little farther than you wanted to go, but you agreed and the Word got pushed back.

And then one day, the Word, as it was originally written, was gone. Not just in America, but globally.

In a 2020 Wallstreet Journal piece, Matthew Taylor King reported that China and its President, Xi Jinping, are trying to reinterpret the Bible to make a more accurate interpretation of core socialist values. He quotes Xi Lian, a professor at Duke University Divinity School, who says the Communist Party wants to "create a new version of Christianity shorn of its transcendent visions and values."

There is no misinterpreting this. We are living in a time of great deception. If earthly authority can't eradicate God's laws and His message of hope, then it will try to alter it to fit their narrative. Again, the message is clear, as it says in Deuteronomy 4:2 *You shall not add to the word which I am commanding you, nor take away from it, that you may keep the commandments of the Lord your God which I command you.*

Revelation 22:18-19 repeats this warning and is very clear about the dire consequences of failing to abide by it, saying *For I testify unto every man that heareth the words of the prophecy of this book, If any man shall add unto these things, God shall add unto him the plagues that are written in this book:*

And if any man shall take away from the words of the book of this prophecy, God shall take away his part out of the book of life, and out of the holy city, and from the things which are written in this book.

There is a time to be silent and there is a time to speak, a time to compromise and, more importantly, a time to stand firm. These times we find ourselves in, the latter in both cases is the better choice. I know you've stepped back and asked *how did we get here? How did injustice go unchecked?* I'll tell you how, apathy, fear and silence subdued our tongues and took over our neighborhoods and churches like a dark cloud. Without Holy Rebels like Martin Luther, the enemy will continue to encroach and perpetuate fear until foundational truth is completely gone.

REBEL WITHOUT A PAUSE

There are two absolutes you can count on for telling the truth about God's Word; somebody's going to hate you for it and somebody will love you for it. That's inevitable. But if you're overly concerned with either one, you're doing it for the wrong reasons.

Out of the abundance of the heart, the mouth speaketh, and now is not the time to be meek nor pause. The world needs more truth tellers, more people who won't bow to culture's intimidation tactics. Public opinion polls seem to agree with that. Heading into the 2020 primaries, an NPR/Marist Poll found that Fifty-two percent of Americans, including a majority of independents, said they are against the country becoming more politically correct and are upset that there are too many things people can't say anymore.

And while this might seem like a fairly recent issue, suppression of the truth has been around much longer than you think. In 1996, Reverend Joe Wright received thousands of calls to his church and his mailbox overflowed with complaints regarding the opening prayer he delivered at a session of the Kansas House of Representatives. What was the big hoopla about? What did he say that got people so fired up and ready to cancel him?

Judge for yourself:

'Woe to those who call evil good,' but that is exactly what we have done. We have lost our spiritual equilibrium and reversed our values. We have exploited the poor and called it the lottery. We have rewarded laziness and called it welfare. We have killed our unborn and called it choice. We have shot abortionists and called it justifiable. We have

neglected to discipline our children and called it building self-esteem.
We have abused power and called it politics. We have coveted our
neighbor's possessions and called it ambition. We have polluted the air
with profanity and pornography and called it freedom of expression.
We have ridiculed the time-honored values of our forefathers and
called it enlightenment. Search us, Oh God, and know our hearts
today; cleanse us from sin and set us free. Amen."

I don't know about you, but to me that sounds like a Holy Rebel delivering some tough medicine to a group of politicians that probably needed it. What might be even better than the actual prayer was Wright's response to the thousands of calls and letters he received criticizing it.

"I'm a preacher at an evangelical church,"he said. "God has called me
to preach the truth. Naturally, any time you preach absolutes, you're
going to offend some people."

The truth is the truth and it stands as truth whether it's God saying it, a pastor saying it or the guy cashing you out at the grocery store saying it. To speak the truth is to challenge those who benefit by the twisting of it.

Do you stop? Do you say: you're going to disagree with me, you're going to criticize me, you're going to engage in conflict with me, you're going to hate and cancel me, so I'll be quiet.

I've been challenged online, asked to curb my opinion by business partners and even shadow banned and censored for "*posting content that goes against community guidelines.*" The powers that be never told me what it was or for how long I'd be canceled but I'll admit, the tactic worked for a bit, it made me pause and rethink what I was doing.

My conscience told me to be bold and speak up for what I knew was right, but fear of castigation was right there as well.

All Scripture is God-breathed and is useful for teaching,
rebuking, correction and training in righteousness
2 Timothy 3:16

The above verse is one of the most important in all of scripture for two reasons: first it tells us that the Bible may have been written by the pen of man but the words come directly from the thoughts of God, and second it tells us that when we obtain its wisdom we should use it for teaching what is right and rebuking that which is wrong.

You should never feel defenseless when you are preaching righteousness, but you will be open for attack. I recalled the words of Peter, in his teachings, warning us there would be scoffers and those following their own evil desires who would not be pleased. It was at this time it became crystal clear to me that I'd been conditioned to fear and that I needed to turn around and put my full trust in God, not man. That doesn't mean getting into theological arguments on a Facebook thread or complaining about the relative who isn't speaking to you because of something you disagreed on, it means to focus your intention on your family and your work in a Godly way. My friend Joel Brown who wrote the foreword to this book said the best thing we can do, as the Body of Christ, is to be about our work. There will always be those who choose to mock and ridicule. Those who write disparaging comments when you stand for your faith. Let that be and be about your work.

"Satan would like nothing better than to have us stop
our ministry and start answering critics,
tracking down lies and malicious stories."
- Reverend Billy Graham

Time spent on those not willing to come to the table is time diverted away from those who are thirsty for wisdom and holding their hands high. It doesn't mean you don't go after those who need it most, but I'm a big believer in the old adage that you save the people swimming toward you first, you control the controllables and keep moving in the direction your spirit is guiding you on your assignment.

EVERYBODY'S TALKIN AT ME

It's human nature to want to fit in and belong to something. We all want to make a difference and have our presence felt. But remember, we have an epidemic of information overload and an abundance of influencers trying to do exactly that, influence us. It's hard to focus and make decisions when everybody's talking at you.

Cable news channels and Instagram handles overflow with angry people yelling and carrying signs. We're in the age of the professional demonstrator as I call it. But what happens when the microphone is put in front of these protestors? They're often so mad and so close minded that they can't articulate a logical argument for what they want and they can only voice what they don't want or what they've been taught to hate.

A cry in anger is often a cry for help, a cry for truth and something to believe in. But we've lost the ability to communicate without anger it seems. Even believers with good intentions can be manipulated by the enemy and enticed by a desire to dominate the conversation.

I remember Angelike and I were heading into a Kiss concert in Nashville one evening. As we entered the building there were two men with bullhorns screaming at people that they would burn in hell for the sin of going to the concert. Angelike looked at me and asked "what do you think their conversion rate is?"

Ironically, we left about 45 minutes into the show because it was extremely dark and full of demonic symbolism, but it was our knowledge of God's Word and discernment that changed our minds, not the men screaming at us outside.

It all leads back to a lack of foundational truth, an absence of teaching that possesses wisdom based on time, nature and morality. That's what it comes down to: we don't have a technology problem, we don't have a left or right problem, instead we have a molarity problem. And that is at the heart of God's Word, moral law. How are we treating one another? Look at the sounds and images on our devices, which are the loudest voices on the news, from Hollywood to D.C., where very few of those voices live up to the moral law they claim to be a proponent of.

Honestly, the devil doesn't care what side you're on, he just wants division. You've heard the phrase it doesn't matter how much you know until you show how much you care. When we lack morality and our actions don't match our words, the enemy wins. He thrives in overwhelm and chaos, and so it is with one last thought from the mind of Tozer that we end this chapter on Holy Rebels, he said *the devil is a better theologian than any of us and is a devil still.*

DID YOU KNOW?

Without The Apostle Paul, there is no Christianity as we know it.

Born in Tarsus, which is now located in Turkey, he was originally known as Saul of Tarsus, a devout Jewish scholar who was highly intelligent and had intimate knowledge of the Old Testament.

Paul was also a Roman citizen who spoke fluid Greek. While in pursuit of followers of Jesus to condemn, even stone, he experienced a miraculous conversion on the Road to Damascus, where he was blinded for three days.

The Lord commanded a man named Ananias to go to Damascus and deliver Paul a message:

Then Ananias went to the house and entered it. Placing his hands on Saul, he said, "Brother Saul, the Lord—Jesus, who appeared to you on the road as you were coming here—has sent me so that you may see again and be filled with the Holy Spirit." Immediately, something like scales fell from Saul's eyes, and he could see again. He got up and was baptized, and after taking some food, he regained his strength.

More Christian theology comes from Paul than any other book in the New Testament. The Book of Romans, which he penned, has had perhaps the greatest impact upon western culture as we know it.

CHAPTER 5

WHAT'S THIS LIFE FOR

"You weren't put here on earth to be remembered;
you were put here to prepare you for eternity"
- Rick Warren

It was the middle of the fall semester, and I was living the dream. Having graduated with a B.A. degree months earlier, I stuck around Tallahassee holding down a job as the doorman at one of the hottest college bars on campus. One night while prepping to open, a conversation sprang up between myself and one of the servers.

He told me about his passion for music and about the band he's put together. I nodded him off rather unimpressed because we had bands play at the bar every night and I hadn't seen or heard of his. Good luck with that, I said as I went to my place at the door.

Years later, as I'm thumbing my way through compact discs (the long boxes) at the music store, I came across the image of a familiar face. It was that same server. He was now the lead singer of the band Creed.

Scott Stapp followed his dream and that's important, because at the core of our human heart, lies passion. Mine is certainly music and I would've done just about anything to be a Rockstar, but a singing voice was not my gift. That doesn't mean I don't follow my passion, I just have to find a different way to incorporate it.

In one of Creed's most popular songs, that former waiter with the big dreams asks *what's this life for*? It's such a timeless question we've all asked ourselves at one point or another. Stapp would say in an interview it was about depressed kids searching for meaning in life. The substance of the song couldn't be more pertinent to where the world is right now at this present time and where we are right now in this book. Everybody seems to be looking for hope. I myself have looked at Angelike and asked her on many occasions, what are we doing here? The question hits young people and old alike and if we can't answer it, then there really isn't much hope.

To give you a clue as to where victory lies, I'll go back to that song and cap it off with one of the most profound things Jesus said during his sermon on the mount. The song ends with the lyrics *We all live under the reign of one king* (Jesus Christ.) All this other political noise about Presidents and Governors and Mayors is just that, noise. As important as they say every election is, the one true leader never falls off of his throne. From Cleopatra to Donald Trump, they come and go, but they can't save you. No matter how much earthly authority presumes to care for you, they can't, at least not like God does, because they don't know you as intimately as your maker does. But I understand, I'm guilty of putting all my thoughts on them (earthly authorities) at times. I'm guilty of giving them dominion over my mind quite regularly. It's attention misplaced. In his Sermon on the Mount Jesus says *for where your treasure is, there your heart will be also.* At the core of this culture war is the question, who or what are we putting in front of Jesus?

The origin of the prefix anti- and its variant ant- is an ancient Greek word which means "against" or "opposite." The Antichrist is a person prophesied in the Book of Revelation who is supremely evil or against everything that Jesus is about, so anything we put in between ourselves and Jesus is a win for him. In a much less sinister but equally dangerous way, the term anti Christ can apply to anything we allow to steal our joy or the spirit of God within us. Pornography is anti Christ. Drug addiction is anti Christ. The evening news can be anti Christ if it steals your joy and takes your eyes off of him. Even something as innocent and rewarding as work can be anti Christ if it distracts us from putting our family and putting God first.

How long will you simple ones love simplicity? and the scorners
delight in their scorning, and fools hate knowledge?
Proverbs 1:22

In my life, I've failed many times and I know I will always be locked in a battle. It's man's sin nature and we never truly overcome it, we war against it. It's not a finish line until it's over, meaning the last breath. Until then, it'll always be our willingness to fight sin and to course correct when we are aware of it. We've spoken a lot so far about cancel culture and how bad it is, but sometimes we need to cancel the things that we put between us and God?

A FEARLESS SOUL

What are you aware of that you resist changing for God because it's just uncomfortable? Being naive means to show a lack of experience or knowledge. For the majority of my adult life, I was naive. I made both mistakes, I looked in the wrong direction for the right reasons and then the right direction for the wrong reasons but the one thing I was unwilling to part with was being comfortable. The enemy knows this.

Do you recall what I said made the biggest difference? Presence. I began putting myself around the right people, those after God's heart, for the right reasons, and in turn, I began seeking His heart more earnestly as well. Let me tell you a story that might help you understand better.

One day I was walking with a friend in Franklin, Tennessee. He was a very successful doctor and business coach. He said to me, "recently I was asked by a spiritual mentor how many people I'd saved at work. I assumed he meant my medical practice, so I asked him, 'like physically save them right?' Yes and No, the mentor replied. Yes, those who come into your practice need help healing their body but what about their souls? How many people who come to see you have you "saved?"

This man was asking my doctor friend to evangelize and spread the healing Word of God to the people who came into his medical practice, his very secular office, seeking help with their bodies.

This was somewhat revolutionary for me to hear. It was bold, almost shocking, to my ears but at the same time, it made sense. As

Christians we often play it safe and even the most passionate believers wear one coat at home and another at work. Let's face it, society expects us to work that way. But still that wasn't the most profound thing he'd say that day.

As we walked further, he turned to me and said "Is God enough for you?" I hesitated and thought, is this a trick question? How am I supposed to answer that?

"What do you mean?" I asked.

"Is God enough? It's a simple question" he replied. "One day God asked me 'Am I enough', and now I'm asking you."

And again, something resonated in my spirit saying "yes" that's a great question. Is God enough?

In this psychological war of vanity and significance and achievement, we have to ask ourselves, what will it really take to satisfy ourselves on a soul level. Once the worldly goal is achieved, how long before you ask yourself, what's next? How long before you say, well, that didn't really satisfy me for that long? When will I ever be truly happy?

I'LL BE HAPPY WHEN...

It's a familiar phrase, isn't it? These four words usually precede a litany of reasons why we are not. We all think we have the answer to this question, don't we? Do me a favor and fill in how that sentence ends for you.

I'll be happy when:

I can get in these jeans.

I get 10,000 followers.

I can get this house clean.

I can get a new car.

I get to retire and move to somewhere warm.

My candidate wins the election.

Regardless of what the answer is, they all have something in common. They are palpable or tangible things: an election, a car, a home, a meal and even a body. Christian author John Eldredge says, **"As long as our happiness is tied to the things we can lose, we are vulnerable."** This is something deep down inside that we all know and it scares us, yet for some reason we're still willing to gamble on it. We're still willing to pour the bulk of our energy into tangible things, which can be taken away or lost. We got a glimpse of that when the pandemic hit and our world appeared to be falling apart as each new month, something else was taken away and we realized how much our happiness was tied to things.

People were afraid to die, which is understandable. Nobody wants to die, but we all will, whether it be from a pandemic or 100 years from now of old age, who knows. What's wrong is that we pour more energy into fear and the avoidance of death than we do into the pursuit of God's word and what it says about how to achieve eternal life. That is where true freedom is found. **Though it costs you all you have, get wisdom.** I repeat that again because with God's wisdom is the truth that will set you free from worrying so much about all those other things.

In our short attention span world, we're all looking for that one-liner, that one quote or sound bite that strikes a chord in our spirit and resonates within all of us. They're out there, the world has no shortage of them, but I was told something once that falls along those lines that truly changed my entire perspective toward the Bible and I'm hoping it might do the same for you. I was told by a very wise man of faith that **God doesn't just want you to know the book of the Lord, but rather the Lord of the book.** Meaning, he's relational and craves connection. That's why I stress so emphatically that it's not just about ritual prayers or about obeying his laws, it's about connection. Right now the big thing the world needs is a reminder of the truth concerning God's nature and the desires of His heart.

The counsel of the LORD stands forever,
the plans of his heart to all generations
(Psalm 33:11)

Like Prince sang, forever is a mighty long time, but there is something else. That something he sang of does in fact include God's plans and it has been extended to all generations, past and present.

This is a foundational piece of wisdom that I lacked. I just had the bits and pieces of faith, without the whole story. I had no perspective. It's like somebody using only two or three moments of your life to explain the whole you, your entire existence. There's no context. So when we begin to uncover God's nature by reading about Him in the full context, then we can begin to see clearly some of the misrepresentations and falsities culture, and even religion, have created. Better yet, it's when you'll begin to sleep better and step into creation on a completely new level.

Forever can be a very scary word for us humans. I contemplated it at a very young age and my daughter, at right about that same age, 10, is when she began to contemplate it too. It's about this age that we begin to comprehend death and our own mortality, maybe not everybody as intensely, but nobody escapes the thought.

Without the Word, how can we explain it? What other document, so widely accepted and so well known, can summarize what this life is for? It is with the Word, literally, that the world began, God spoke the universe and all that is in it into existence. It's the very first line of the Bible, Genesis 1:1 *In the beginning God created the Heavens and the Earth.* Jesus's best friend John, reiterates this in the very first sentence of his gospel, John 1:1 *In the beginning was the Word, and the Word was with God, and the Word was God.*

In the middle of the Bible, in one of Jesus' most memorable lessons, the significance of the Word is highly emphasized as He tells Satan that *it is written we do not live by bread alone, but by every word that proceedeth out of the mouth of God.* (Matthew 4:4). This is an exact confirmation of what Moses told us at the beginning of the Bible. (Deuteronomy 8:3).

And finally, the bookend, another reference to the significance of the Word. It's a line not there by happenstance or chance, but as punctuation.

The last enemy to be destroyed is death. For he "has put everything under his feet." (First Corinthians 15:25) When Satan's time nears the end, Jesus returns with a battle call to overthrow the lawless one *with the breath of his mouth.* (2 Thessalonians 2:8).

Yes, in the very end, it is not weapons, like guns or tanks or even fire, which Jesus uses to defeat the Antichrist and his army, but the Word.

RUACH & ROLL

So what about your personal fight? The daily struggle to find prosperity. If you've felt "less-than-alive" at any time recently, there are two things you need to know: one, you are still breathing and two, you have access to the most creative force in the history of the earth, words.

You might be thinking, really? Words? Yes, with words we possess the ability to speak life into things as well as the ability to drain life from them. I recall a pastor who said the dumbest thing he'd ever heard was the old phrase "sticks and stones may break my bones but words will never hurt me." He said words inflict the most damage. They start wars and end marriages. How can you say they aren't hurtful?

Words are powerful and they possess the potential to conceive, build, shape, heal, mend, improve, regenerate and restore. They are life-giving.

Charles Capps, author of the *The Tongue, A Creative Force* said, *"words are the most powerful thing in the universe."* He describes them as *"containers which we build our life, our future with. They contain faith and fear. The word of God conceived in the heart, formed in the tongue, and spoken out of the mouth is creative power."*

But what is the one thing we need in order to speak them?

Breath. You can't have speech without breath.

Ruach (pronounced roo-akh) is a fascinating Hebrew word used 400 times in the old testament. What's so fascinating about it you ask? For starters, it represents everything you've ever read any book for or attended any conference hoping to get; wisdom, hope, faith, willpower. It's everything that motivates, inspires, stimulates, influences or activates. To put it succinctly, ruach represents your life force, it's God's spirit found in our spirit, and if you want to love and prosper in ways you never imagined, you need to know about it.

And the Lord God formed man of the dust of the ground,
and breathed into his nostrils the (RUACH) breath of life;
and man became a living soul.
Genesis 2:7

How many yoga classes have you been to, how many seminars have you attended where you were instructed to find or get in touch with your breath? Question, did the teacher ever tell you why, other than physiologically of course, that there was such power in your breath?

They tend to leave that part out most of the time.

Ruach Elohim, (Hebrew for the *Breath of God*), is life-giving, like the breath we take into our lungs by inhaling and exhaling. Questions about where we get breath and how we come to think, feel and love are answered in Genesis 2:7 when Adam came to life by means of the ruach being breathed by God into his lifeless body. In our daily walk, we not only need breath to speak with but in a deeper sense, to create with. This is why we need to go deeper here and why the term ruach is so important, it is very literally our life force. In the Greek of the New Testament, the word is often referred to as pneuma. *"Verily, verily, I say unto thee, Except a man be born of water and of the Spirit (pneuma), he cannot enter into the kingdom of God."* John 3:5.

Breath is synonymous with sustaining life on earth and receiving the breath of the Holy Spirit (Ruach), as in this scripture, is synonymous with everlasting life.

Of course, if it's not God's breath, or ruach, that brought you to life then yes, by all means, you have permission to spend the rest of your time here on earth worrying about your inadequacies, lingering in fear of rejection from the world and living out your days in mediocrity.

In Genesis 1 it says the earth was formless and empty, in a state of chaos. This is how so many people I've coached describe themselves to me. In a state of internal chaos. Remember in chapter one, what did I say was the number one cause of self sabotage amongst the executives I surveyed? Overwhelm right? And what was one of the primary consequences of that overwhelm? An inability to focus and make decisions. Genesis then says that the spirit of God (Ruach Elohim) hovered over the waters and what's next is the most consequential thing that ever happened...EVER! God said *let there be light* and it broke the darkness and God called it good. It's important to note that this was day one, and that God didn't create light (the sun) to separate day from night, until day four. This light on day one is the spirit, the spark. It was spoken with breath, ruach, the creative force. That same spirit, ruach, of God is hovering over each one of us and it can break your chaos, pierce your darkness and bring you to life just like it did the earth and Adam. The Holy Spirit has been referred to by many theologians as the most underutilized force in the universe.

To everything there is a divine order, God's breath helped bring order to the chaos and then it became the source of creation through his Word. We were created to create and I believe with all my heart that we are invited, by the Holiest of Holies, to co-create with him.

The devil is an interrupter. He wants to be an author,
but heaven never gave him a pen. So he can read your story,
but he can't write your story.
Pastor John Gray

This is a time to embrace creation, to take that pen God gave you and write. If a young person came to me and asked for a blueprint to success, I would advise them to find ways to tap into their creativity. It is both spiritual and practical.

According to a global survey by Adobe Data, 60 percent of CEOs polled cited *creativity* as the most important leadership quality. It also said that 75 percent of people think they are not living up to their creative potential. As my wife Angelike says, these people are missing their "*spiritual back office*" or their ability to co-create with God right here and now to make an impact in this world, right here and now.

It's not a secret, this power was not supposed to be kept from you. It's right there in black and white. We are described as God's handiwork, created in his own image, his breath interchangeable with ours in order that we may harness it to co-create with wisdom, hope, faith and courage. In order to motivate, inspire, stimulate, influence and activate for the purpose that we bring victory to the kingdom of God.

Do you not know that in a race all the runners run,
but only one gets the prize?
Run in such a way as to get the prize.
1 Corinthians 9:24

When I think of racing, I think of sprinters, but I think of horses and I also think of cars. Now with sprinters and horses, we know they use breath, but cars? Let me tell you an interesting story about breathing air as it relates to competition and one which I feel is an excellent metaphor for ruach or pneuma and what it means to God's desire for you to experience success in this life.

In 1988, NASCAR mandated restrictor plates in the engines of all cars at Daytona and Talladega speedways. It was a sincere effort to improve driver safety by slowing cars down. But, one problem, it had the opposite effect. A byproduct of "plate racing" was a more hazardous situation in which cars stayed bunched in packs, producing even more violent multi-car wrecks.

In February of 2019, after 30 years after restrictor plates, the final race using these restrictor plates was held at the Daytona 500.

As one NASCAR expert put it, no plates means more driver control, greater passing ability, less hazardous drafting and more room to maneuver between cars. I find it an interesting parallel. Consider how the NASCAR restrictor plates worked, the device limited the flow of air to the car's engine, thereby reducing the horsepower and, consequently, the speed the engine can generate power.

Spiritually speaking, this is the same thing culture and the influence of small gods has on the Body of Christ. Culture is trying to reduce our intake of the ruach, our intake of God's breath, thereby reducing the power and speed at which we can create with it. They take God out of the public so, like NASCAR, everybody is safer, but what's happened? Just the opposite. It's been way more dangerous.

Do not allow the fear of man to take away your ability to maneuver through this life with all the power and speed God has made available to you. Like Paul says, compete to win your race. If others don't want you to try, if they say, play it safe, just tone it down; don't agree to it. Don't go to the track with a watered down version of your talent or what you know to be true because culture is trying to get you to play by its rules, for the "greater good" so nobody's feelings get hurt.

I'd like to think Paul and even Jesus would agree that when you wrap your identity in Kingdom work and you have Kingdom fuel, and get out there and win, it's what you were made for.

Get out there and change the world!

DID YOU KNOW?

We don't just have evidence of Jesus and his works from his disciples or from biblical authors but from secular historians of his time as well. The most popular of which is Josephus.

Josephus was a first century Roman scholar and historian born in 37 AD who is widely accredited and respected for his attention to detail and factual reporting. He writes *"At this time, there was a wise man who was called Jesus. And his conduct was good, and he was known to be virtuous. And many people from among the Jews and other nations became his disciples.*

In many ways, Josephus was a war correspondent as well as a historian. His job was to report the facts, unbiased and uninhibited, from battle scenes.

And when I was sent by Titus Caesar with Cerealins, and a thousand horsemen, to a certain village called Thecoa, in order to know whether it were a place fit for a camp, as I came back, I saw many captives crucified, and remembered three of them as my former acquaintance.

In addition, Josephus gives historical verification to crucifixion of Jesus in particular.

He writes, *Now there was about this time Jesus, a wise man, for he was a doer of wonderful works, a teacher. He drew over to him both many of the Jews and many of the Gentiles. And when Pilate, at the suggestion of the principal men amongst us, had condemned him to the cross, those that loved him at the first did not forsake him; And the tribe of Christians, so named from him, are not extinct at this day.*

If nothing else, this puts a source outside of the Bible as a witness to both the practice of crucifixion and to the fact that a man named Jesus was condemned to die by Pontius Pilate, the 5th Governor of Judaea.

CHAPTER 6

THE CHOSEN

"There seemed to sound a voice which I thought I distinctly heard, and most certainly understood, which said to me, "Go preach the Gospel!" I immediately replied aloud, "No one will believe me." Again I listened, and again the same voice seemed to say "Preach the Gospel; I will put words in your mouth, and will turn your enemies to become your friends."
- Jarena Lee

If you think you're tired of *waiting on the world to change*, John Mayer must be exhausted. In 2006, in his hit song of the same title, he sang there was a problem with those who lead it (the world), but he just didn't feel like we had the means to rise above and beat it.

That's why John Mayer sings pop songs and not worship music.

As for me, I'm neither a waiter nor a wisher, meaning I haven't tossed a coin in a fountain or blown out the candles on a birthday cake with any degree of expectation since I was a kid. I am a believer though and I'm going to assume that's one of the reasons you chose to pick up this book, because you're a believer too or at least looking for something to believe in. In that case, let's agree on what was spoken in the last chapter, that we are equipped, that we have the power to create a better reality not just in our own lives, but for the world.

Man's authority and instruction doesn't appear to be the answer to what we've been looking for. Man says just print more money. Man says pass the bill so we can then see what's in it. Man says put this potion in your body without questioning it. Man says true love is when a guy in a tuxedo picks a woman from a cattle call and hands her a rose.

Is any of that producing fruit so far? How long do we have to try this experiment that asks God to play second string quarterback before we put him back in as the starter?

Do me a favor and go back to your childhood for a moment. Perhaps it was a time at school or maybe in the park by your house, but regardless we all have that moment when we sat there in line waiting to be picked by team captains.

I see now, a lot of those same faces I saw as a child. The same postures too. There was always an ultra confident kid with his feet square and his arms folded knowing he would go first. There was the freak of nature kid who was shaving and wearing size 11 shoes at 10. Those two, and the kid who brought the ball, were always shoo-ins to get picked.

And then there was everybody else.

The overly-anxious kid with his hand up, waiving it furiously mimicking *pick me, pick me* with his mouth. There was the kid who was just kinda oblivious to reality, both shoes untied, two different socks, looking behind his shoulder at the dog in the neighbors yard. You'd have to repeat his name twice because he never heard it the first time. And then there was the small, skinny kid whose gray tee hung off his shoulders as if it were still on the hanger. His legs crossed at the ankles as he stood with one hand folded under his armpit and the other one nervously biting his fingernails hoping, for just once, that he was not last to go. And then there was always somebody's little brother, who was way off to the side, so tired of getting his hopes up and told to get away that he stopped bothering to get in the line up at all.

My next question is, when you lay in bed at night, alone with your thoughts, do you feel like any of those kids? Do you feel like you're on the verge of getting picked and making an impact or are you asking yourself *am I just here playing the game, taking up space?*

The fear of not being chosen, in today's world shows up as *you didn't get many likes, you weren't asked to speak at the conference or lead the call, you didn't get invited to the party* or *you aren't vaccinated.*

Once again we see how becoming irrelevant or anonymous feeds into our fear of isolation. It's a tool of the enemy who would like nothing better than for you to feel like nobody wanted you or that you were irrelevant. That's why being canceled is such a deterrent to so many who want to speak up but don't. It's also why significance by any means is such an allure to people on social media. Whether it's the guy risking his life doing some dangerous stunt on YouTube or the girl flaunting her bodyparts all over Instagram, everyone seems to be begging to be acknowledged in some outward way because they are lacking the knowledge of who loves them on the inside.

People are suffering in a society that really reverted back to grade school rather than progressed, or evolved, into anything more. So we talk about building a tribe while posting the hustle quote and that checks off the confidence box, but is it actually foundational? Can you build a spiritual home on that or is it just a temporary win?

Let me pause right here. Some of you may think I'm pointing fingers, making broad accusations. If I humble myself, I can honestly say that I write these words because I'm in this battle with you. Just like you, I live it, I see it, I hear it and have those same apprehensions and doubts and wonder like you, if I'll be chosen to matter, chosen to be important, chosen to be seen as valuable.

Maybe you'll let your guard down a minute and search your spirit asking yourself if the artificial replacements we've made for God and His love have made their way into your life without you realizing it. The enemy and his counterfeit affection, his earthly idolatry, is calling many who are lost, and that call is loud. Think about how much of our day, how much of our thoughts and public discourse are influenced by the need for attention and the praise of significance from things other than God and from the people under our own roof.

Because the internet has made our world feel so big, it can easily make us feel quite small. Whereas our mothers and fathers worried about their place amongst the community on their street, we now worry about our status amongst the community of the world. Our parents were highly satisfied with three close friends in the neighborhood, but we need 10,000 people spread across the globe to feel loved now.

Sure, I'm making some assumptions or again, painting with a broad stroke, but it can't be denied, I'm not greatly exaggerating. I know this for a fact because I've studied it. I've spoken to and coached thousands of people who are experiencing this need to fit in and feel chosen. A need to feel seen and validated. This is a real problem facing our country.

During our time in Nashville, Angelike and I became acquainted with a couple of kindred spirits, Josh and Christi Straub whose mission is similar to ours. They are the founders of *Famous At Home* and their mission is to help those who thrive with attention and identity outside the home to focus on putting more effort on the stage inside their home. They say it's often the family which gets the leftovers in this busy world of hustle and that the remedy *all starts by realizing that the greatest red carpet you'll ever walk is through your front door because your biggest fans are the ones under your own roof.*

That is a noble cause that I think the world would benefit greatly by paying more attention to. And please don't misunderstand my position, I know God wants us to be about our work. We are given ambitious spirits to run the race, but the key is to run OUR race, on a track that God laid out for us specifically. So the message, whether it's mine and Angelike's or couples like the Straubs, is not to forget the world, but to remember God's divine order by not allowing a values inversion to let your work mission subvert power or attention away from the greatest mission He has called us to, family.

A SACRED IDENTITY

Do you think most people walking around today are cognizant of their identity? Has the pervasiveness of social media created an identity crisis in our minds? It seems fairly obvious to me, in my studies, that it has. Culture will try to group you into one of two categories, either you're a somebody or a nobody. You either matter or you don't. You're an influencer or a follower, chosen by culture or rejected by it. Blending in or standing out.

If that's the case, when you see somebody who appears to possess a worldly prosperity or a massive online presence, you might just assume that God chose to work with them over you, that he listened to their prayer over yours? But the Apostle Paul tells us *if anyone loves God, he is known by God.* The psalmist David says our book is written by Him, every one of our days authored.

If you watched the series *The Chosen*, then you'll recall at the end of the first episode is one of the most powerful scenes that any movie has ever interpreted from Scripture. Mary Magdalene is walking out of a tavern and Jesus calls to her *Mary of Magdalene.* She immediately stops in her tracks, drops the cup she is holding and asks *who are you?*

Jesus says *thus says the Lord who created you, fear not for I have called you by name, you are mine.*

I must've watched that scene at least a dozen times and in every single instance, the hair on my arms stands up and my eyes become overwhelmed with tears. It's powerful to see with your eyes what you've only read about before in scripture.

The scripture is from Isaiah 43:1 and it's one of the most important of all those in the Bible for us to wrap our heads around. To think that God knows us intimately and by name is heart-stirring. So much so, it's easy to go into skeptic mode.

Me? Really? How could God know me?

David says God has authored every one of our days to which again you could be a skeptic and say, "really, even the boring days or the bad days? God wrote those? Was he in a bad mood or low on creativity when he penned them? And what about my pain and heartbreak. God wrote those too, huh? That's not very nice."

This is where our human minds wander into doubt and negativity. This is when our faith gets rattled without knowledge and context of the Word. It tells us we will have trouble, but that's in this world, where the enemy has free reign and we have free will. The very next line reassures us, *but take heart, I have overcome the world.*

The point is, there is *more* than this world. There is more to us (our spirit) than the eighty-something years of earthly life expectancy. Imagine our time here on earth being something like the first second of the first day of first grade and eternity would look something like our entire schooling, all the way through college. Our time here pales in comparison to the bigger picture.

So maybe things aren't happening as you'd hoped or prayed for right now and it's convenient to blame somebody other than yourself. But never forget in the dark what God told us in the light. On those "boring" or "tough" days when you're trying to look at your life and make sense of it through the lens of culture, judging yourself by likes, comments or somebody else's reality which you think must be better, remember you are chosen.

Everyday doesn't have to be post-worthy and ego-feeding. When we lose ourselves in entertainment (device distraction) or feel-good consumption (food or alcohol) in the hopes of helping to forget what isn't perfect, remember you are chosen.

When you go to the bookstore or Amazon to order that next book to help you get out of the funk, I want you to remember the original instructions that told us how we first got in it. The battle is not new. It started in the Garden when Eve was not happy with what she was given (an entire garden of Paradise) and was deceived into focusing on that which she didn't have (the fruit of the Tree of Knowledge). What have you been given, children, a home, even your eyes and legs, that you're overlooking because you're too busy being tempted by looking at what you don't have. That which you've been deceived into believing is more fulfilling. Like the fruit of the forbidden tree, it's not yours to covet.

Free will broke this world of its innocence and since that day man has been pursued by both sides, the enemy who says keep searching this world for satisfaction and God who tells us to set our minds on things above.

I know what you're thinking, I've heard that before and it sounds nice but unfortunately I wake up each day on earth, not heaven, so can you give me something I can incorporate into my daily life, here and now?

Absolutely, I'm going to because Angelike warned me when writing this, if you're just gonna tell people to be happy with what they have, that's not a book, it's a post, and by the way, it's been said a million times.

She was spot on and there's no way I'd do that to you. The Pursuit is all about thinking bigger, loving bigger and taking on a view of prosperity that is life changing. But first things first, the world is broken and we do reside in it, so to believe we will not face trial and heartache is unrealistic. Second, and more important, to believe that your maker would create you but then choose not to co-create with you is a deception that's simply not true.

There is a divine order and when we honor it, we find His favor. Success is in direct accordance with obedience to His Word. Just look at Genesis, everything that came to be in Creation was "good" because it obeyed His Word.

Paul, while in prison, writes a letter to the Ephesians telling them to *live a life worthy of the calling they have received*. He says *in Him (Christ) we were also chosen*. It indicated that we are *included* when we hear the *message of Truth*. Isiah's scripture reads:

"Bring my sons from afar and my daughters from the ends of the earth- everyone who is called by my name, whom I created for my glory, whom I formed and made."

Wow, if that isn't a beautiful invitation to stop running from Him, to stop begging for the attention and approval of the world and instead turn around and wrap your head around the fact that the creator of the Universe knows your name and that you belong to him, that He is highly invested in your success and happiness, in relation to Him, not apart from Him.

HEAD GAMES

Anybody who has raised children knows that they crave one thing above all else, attention. Even the sweetest little toddler, when deprived of attention, will act up. They cry or throw things around trying to be noticed in hopes of getting mom or dad's affection. This doesn't change as we get older, human nature is to crave attention. It's a basic human need. Anybody who has gone through a basic psychology course in school might recall renowned psychologist Abraham Maslow and his famous Hierachy of Needs triangle. His theory was that human beings can only self actualize (achieve their full potential) after basic physiological and safety needs are met. Once those are met, he said one can then focus on seeking belonging, self-esteem and love. Belongingness, refers to a human emotional need for interpersonal relationships, connectedness, and being part of a group. Self-esteem being a desire for respect and status and love should be self explanatory.

How we go about achieving those things is certainly influenced by our environment, our culture. This brings us to another great thought by author John Eldredge who said, *"We think we have to keep doing something in order to be desirable. Once we find something that will bring us some attention, we have to keep it going or risk the loss of the attention. And so we live with the fear of not being chosen and the burden of maintaining whatever it is about us that might get us noticed and the commitment never to be seen for who we really are."*

I've raised three children and can tell you from experience, even before they can walk or talk, they can figure out how to get your attention, and once they know that, you can bet it will be repeated. This begs the question, what is a culture with less scripture and more screen time doing to our sense of self-worth and the desire to feel chosen? Caroline Miller, Editorial Director of the Child Mind Institute penned an article about the effects of social media on young people. In it, Dr. Jerry Bubrick, a Clinical Psychologist at the Child Mind Institute said, "kids spend so much time on social media trying to post what they think the world will think is a perfect life. Look at how happy I am! Look how beautiful I am! Without that they're worried that their friends won't accept them. They're afraid of being rejected." And if they are getting positive feedback from their social media accounts, they might worry that what their friends like isn't the "real" them.

Isn't that interesting. If you recall earlier talking about wanting to know the rest of the story, is the person we follow or celebrity we admire truly that blissful and happy? Every time we touch a screen and log onto our social media account, whether we're cognizant of it or not, we're being programmed to seek attention, to be "chosen" by our peers or audience. It's not a generational thing, it's a universal thing of our era, and it only stands to get more significant.

Early in 2022, I personally interviewed dozens of teenagers between the ages of 13 and 19. To my surprise, they were, for the most part, well aware of the addiction facing them and recognized a need to balance or police their screen time. Even more interesting was their reaction when I asked "how do you feel about being judged?" The question, almost always elicited a visceral reaction, and by in large, they all said it affected them negatively and they didn't like it.

So here we are, we've arrived at this point in history in which we've been conditioned to crave the attention and significance offered by culture so much that it's consuming much of our thoughts and impacting our happiness. It's like this huge tsunami we all see gaining momentum but feel helpless to stop. Isn't it paradoxical that we will scratch and claw to get more attention, more followers, even pay big sums of money to purchase acceptance, but for one reason or another, we don't feel it's worthy to pursue, with that same vigor, the attention of the one who knit us in our mother's womb?

I say this in humility because I've done it, be it through fancy watches, fancy cars, or campaigns to get more followers, I've tried to fill my spirit via things. I've pursued the adoration of the world in an attempt to gain significance in it. And there was God, the entire time, waving His arms saying pursue me with an equal enthusiasm so you will stop being so thirsty for things that can never satisfy you by their nature. Like Jesus told the woman at the well, *whoever drinks the water I give them will never thirst. Indeed, the water I give them will become in them a spring of water welling up to eternal life.*

So, yes, I can confirm what Eldredge says, I can tell you from first hand experience, trying to keep up with something you are not, is an exhausting 24-hour-a-day job, and yet still, so many people are trying to live their lives like a reality show with this massive pressure to be like everybody else so they can experience validation and acceptance. You know it and I know it. We live in a world where attention (good or bad) and significance (good or bad) has corrupted people who are willing to do anything to feel significant or gain wealth. We've also seen how culture will reward depravity, with more fame and money. While that may never change, you can. You have the ability to decide to be a part of it or to be set apart from it. God invites us to "come out from them and be separate and that He will Father to us" (2 Corinthians 6:17).

Again, what an amazing invitation our Father has made to us. And be it from above or in our homes, any parent knows, their child doesn't have to be perfect in order to receive their affection. Your family are the people you can be yourself around, the ones you don't have to put on a costume for every day. That's how incredibly liberating it is to clothe yourself in a Godly confidence which you cannot be stripped of. One where you're not constantly looking for things to prop you up or filter parts out, but one where you can be you.

It's a choice, I'm sure you feel the pressure to be "known" and to be "significant" in the way we live these days. Because people today, more so than in the past, will change careers several times, it's very common to feel a need to "keep up" in ways other generations didn't have to. The call to be youthful and attractive in order to achieve success and the pull of culture's influences who say just the opposite, you can't get old, you can't relax, you must stay relevant and always be working to grow your influence. If you don't think these things are contributing to higher levels of stress and depression, look a bit closer at the filters and the efforts which go into Facebook and Instagram photos. How many emails and text messages do you receive promising the ability to be more relevant, to get noticed more?

Because of this trend in business culture, most people who Angelike and I work with are going through some sort of transition and they typically possess a sense of urgency to make big changes and make them fast, so they can look like and compete with everybody else. The first thing we find ourselves doing is trying to break them of that mentality. We encourage people to separate themselves from the allure to look and act like everybody else and to get more in tune with who God says they are and what beautiful gifts He has blessed them with that perhaps they aren't seeing. It's hardly ever a big change they need, but rather a hard look in the mirror at what's always been with them all along. Angelike always says, "success, in anything, is on the other side of a tough conversation and many times that conversation starts with us, meaning in our own head."

Each day we wake up we have to be our own motivational coach. But we don't have to do it alone or fake it. We are told that *we are His workmanship, a chosen race, a royal priesthood.* We just have a hard time believing it. I've been there way too many times in my life, lying in bed thinking nobody gets me, nobody understands what's going on in my head, thinking to myself, how am I going to accomplish the things I want to accomplish? Then I begin to panic thinking the clock is ticking, this is no time to rest. Often, out of pure frustration, we just start pushing buttons. It's like when your computer freezes and you just keep hitting return rather than slowing down and taking the time to find out what's happened.

The Word is perfectly situated for a time such as these, a time when we panic, a time when we feel like we're being pulled in a thousand directions, but we don't know which way is up. So when you read *My peace I give you. I do not give to you as the world gives. Do not let your hearts be troubled and do not be afraid,* it's there to do just that, give you peace of mind. Because it's in the moments when we are most vulnerable, when our inner voice or consciousness strives to reconcile our ideal self (who we strive to be) with our actual self (who we are at the moment), that the relationship with the Holy Spirit grows and whispers to be 'be still." It's that quiet time when you are assured that there is indeed somebody who knows you and who you can be yourself with - God. He knows every hair on our head (Luke 12:7) and His thoughts of us would outnumber the grains of sand on the earth (Psalm 139:18).

Yet even with these clear assurances, it's still tempting not to trust Him, to tell ourselves, not me, I'm not on His radar, those are just words in a book. Who am I after all, just one of hundreds of people on the street right now or one of millions of people sending their prayers up at night. There's no way God can know who I am.

Guess what? That doubt, God knew that would come as well and includes a story or anecdote for us. Isn't it crazy how that old book not only knows what will trouble us in our time, but also possesses the foresight to predict our excuses and see two steps ahead.

THE PROPHET WITHOUT HONOR

In Mark's Gospel there is a story, which upon first read, might satisfy the skeptic in you, but when we look deeper, it should do just the opposite, and that is to cement everything else you've read about faith. In this story, Jesus, in the middle of his ministry, returns to his hometown of Nazarath, where the people there knew him and his family very well. They'd heard of his wisdom and ability to perform wonders, yet he was unable to perform any miracles there. So at an initial glance it's easy to say, here is the all powerful Jesus who was unable to perform miracles in his hometown, why should we believe in a man who failed amongst the people who knew him best?

But wait, ask yourself is faith a one way street, is it a magic potion or is it a relationship of trust and belief? Seventeenth century theologian Matthew Poole writes this concerning the lesson of the Prophet Without Honor; *(Jesus) divine doctrine was so convincing, and the fame of his glorious works done in places near them was so universal and credible, that there was just cause of his rational wonder that they did not believe.* In other words, Jesus' power was incumbent upon their willingness to meet him and believe. Belief is a word used over 100 times in the New Testament. Saint Augustine articulates this perfectly when he says *without God, we cannot, and without us, He will not.*"

Angelike and I use the story of The Prophet Without Honor in our coaching ministry because, like Jesus, many people are rendered powerless in their ability to create change or revival in their own lives because of the disbelief aimed at them by their closest friends and family members. We call them the scoffers, or those who are closed off to believing because they are rooted in skepticism. For instance they may see or hear that you're going back to school or that you plan to take on a new career, and because they feel they know you so well, they cast doubt in your ability to do something different that what they're accustomed to in the old you. So you couldn't possibly change their belief about you because in their heads, they lack faith in you, but more importantly, they often lack faith overall.

Belief is powerful and it's something taught in secular self development every day across the world, but it's often belief in oneself, absent of God. One of my favorite Pastors, Mark Driscoll, makes this very poignant observation about this type of culture, "*In the world we live, it is common for people to honor, to value, to esteem and to pursue pride and arrogance, so much so that we use words like self-esteem, self improvement, self-actualization and self-help. All of those are different ways of saying I can take care of me, I don't need Him (God) and there is a pride to that.*"

Maybe this resonates with you, maybe you've experienced this doubt in your own ability to change or in God's ability to help you change that your faith is shot, just like the scoffers in Nazareth. I urge you, don't give up, sometimes it's what we can't see that ultimately brings us the most faith.

Let me explain. Was there ever a time when you put so much prayer and hope into that magic moment when everything would change, but nothing happened? Was there a time when you desired an epiphany or breakthrough but didn't get it? Or maybe it just didn't happen when you wanted it to. Is it bad to suggest that perhaps you were disappointed in God? I don't know, I suppose that's part of human nature when you don't know his heart.

I've experienced this gap in faith. On one hand, I was a doubter, meaning sure I prayed, but without belief, almost like purchasing a lottery ticket that you don't really expect to win. Only God's word is not a game of chance, it's a guarantee. On the other hand, what I prayed for was not in my best interest. I was looking in the right direction (God) for the wrong things, things the world was telling me were important. Things which I would later discover would not have been in my best interest. For example, I prayed for the love of a woman who looked good to the world but was lacking a heart for God and I prayed to land a job that paid well and was prestigious, but was not in line with my ethos or my calling. Thankfully, let me repeat that, thankfully, I did not get what I thought I wanted, the Lord had more in store for me that I couldn't see.

It's with that in mind that I say to you, imagine for a moment that God is trying to break through, asking you questions like will the timelines you've placed on me pull you farther away from the plans I have for you or, are you going to trust my plan so we can co-create something magnificent, something that lasts? Imagine God asking you, do you realize amongst all the noise and all the overwhelm that you experience, that I'm still focused on you, begging for your attention, that I'm aware of you and like a loving father, I want to help you because I've chosen you. All you have to do is choose me back.

DID YOU KNOW?

Did you know that 1,000 years before Jesus was crucified on the cross, King David prophesied the occurrence in Psalm 22:16-18.

Dogs surround me, a pack of villains encircles me;
they pierce my hands and my feet.
All my bones are on display; people stare and gloat over me.
They divide my clothes among them and cast lots for my garment.

This prophecy predicted Roman crucifixion before it was even invented. The day of fulfillment occurred in Jerusalem around 33 AD as Jesus was executed by the Romans at Golgotha, a skull-shaped hill in ancient Jerusalem. This is referred to in all four Gospels (Matthew 27:33, Mark 15:22, Luke 23:33, and John 19:17):

(On dividing Jesus's garments)

And when they had crucified him,
they parted his garments, casting lots upon them
Mark 15:24

(On Jesus's bones not be broken which is repeated by Moses in Numbers 9:12 when he wrote of the sacrificial lamb *"They shall leave none of it til morning, nor break one of it's bones"*

Then came the soldiers, and broke the legs of the first, and of the other which was crucified with him. But when they came to Jesus, and saw that he was dead already, they brake not his legs
John 19:32-33.

(On the piercing of Jesus's hands)

(Thomas said) Unless I see the nail marks in his hands and put my finger where the nails were, and put my hand into his side, I will not believe."
A week later his disciples were in the house again, and Thomas was with them. Though the doors were locked, Jesus came and stood among them and said, "Peace be with you!" Then he said to Thomas, "Put your finger here; see my hands. Reach out your hand and put it into my side. Stop doubting and believe."
John 20: 24-27

The Jews did their executions by stoning, the Romans did them by crucifixion. That determined the method of Jesus' death: He would hang on a tree—a cross made of wood.

Deuteronomy 21:22

And if a man have committed a sin worthy of death, and he be to be put to death, and thou hang him on a tree: His body shall not remain all night upon the tree, but thou shalt in any wise bury him that day; (for he that is hanged is accursed of God;)

The Bible doesn't say, "Cursed is everyone who is stoned." It says, "Cursed is everyone who hangs on a tree." A curse inflicted by God, which the transgressor (Jesus) is made to endure.

CHAPTER 7
YOU DON'T KNOW MY NAME

In the total expanse of human life there is not a single
square inch of which the Christ, who alone and sovereign,
does not declare, "that is mine!"
- Abraham Kuype

As I mentioned, much of my twenties were spent working as a doorman at different bars and clubs, not only in college but while beginning my journalism career in South Florida. Writer by day, doorman by night. That was my life. The commonality between the two was that I heard great stories any time I went to work. While the newspaper stories were always straightforward and entertaining, they were nothing compared to the narratives I heard from people trying to skip the line at the entrance to the club. The improvisation and drama which came from the party goers who had a few drinks in them was both inventive and hysterical.

The point here, and it can be a polarizing one, is when you reach the door, will you be drunk on idolatry and the knowledge of gods (small g) trying to talk your way into the Kingdom of Heaven or will you be secure in your passage because you knew the truth of God and lived your life accordingly.

It's a polarizing question because anytime we talk about who gets into heaven and who doesn't, we must be sensitive to the individual journey on one end, but adherent to sound doctrine on the other. The purpose of this book, and specifically this chapter, is not to try to identify a good person from a bad person, a pious person from an agnostic person or an attempt to say who is and who isn't getting into heaven. Like I said, my intention is never to stand on a soapbox with a bullhorn because that's not a method with great results. My goal is to simply point people back to foundational truth and unmuddy what culture is not only trying to pour dirt on, but attempting to bury, God's Word.

The Bible is under attack. The aim to subvert it, counterfeit it and replace it, can't be ignored. A big player in that counterfeiting and replacing is the push toward New Age wisdom in the form of things like The Secret (manifesting), worship of the universe, paying homage to mother nature, tarot cards and crystals.

In the previous two chapters, we discovered what this life is for and acknowledged that we have been chosen by God, but we have to address the third component that completes the contract, and that is we have to choose God back. It is our free will, as I've mentioned, to accept or deny Him. How can you make an educated choice?

God, the Universe, Source or Whatever You Believe

Years back when Angelike and I were first beginning our business and dipping our toes into the world of self development, we went to a 3-day seminar. As we sat amongst 4,000 or so people pumping their fists and beating their chests, I remember looking around at the enthusiasm in the room and being in awe of the people who were certain their lives would change from that moment on. We were two of them.

While I can't poll those 4,000 people, I'd make a healthy bet that many are still suffering from the same issues they brought into that conference. It's not a knock on the host or the event, but it's a truth about human nature that we stated in chapter one, there are good fixes and quick fixes but few if any, are good, quick fixes. In our culture of wanting it fast and wanting it now, when somebody of stature and great influence tells us what's wrong with us and how to correct it, it's powerful. You tell me though, when that person of great influence talks for fifteen minutes to a woman who has been abused for fifteen years, is that a path for what you'd call foundational change? No, it's a quick fix.

Change is something our world has developed an unhealthy attitude toward. We think we can pay for it with a credit card or simply write down all our fears on a piece of paper and burn them in a group exercise and somehow we're magically fixed. Remember, knowledge is one thing, transformation is another. One is absent of love and the other requires it.

In the last days there will be difficulty,
that people will be lovers of self, lovers of money, slanderous,
reckless and lovers of pleasure rather than lovers of God. People will
have the appearance of godliness, but deny God's power.
2 Timothy 3:5

It's easy to take this verse from Second Timothy and manipulate it into meaning a number of things that can either make an argument true or make it false, but again, let's just use the simple rule of common sense. As for last days, that's up for anybody's guess, and I don't want to go there. But are the other statements relevant to what we see taking place around us? Do we have lovers of self and money who have an appearance of godliness, saying God on one hand but "whatever you believe" on the other, essentially undermining God's authority.

Not to deny the value of such knowledge teachers, but when you deny the Lord his dominion, there is no gray area in scripture for that. And without a reverence for God and without His love taking precedence, the teaching not only lacks foundation, but opens a great door for deception and idolatry.

Have nothing to do with such people. They are the kind who worm
their way into homes and gain control over gullible women, who are
loaded down with sins and are swayed by all kinds of evil desires,
always learning but never able to come to a knowledge of the truth.
2 Timothy 3:5-7

The virtuous influencers of government, Hollywood and social media technically aren't denying God right? True, but this is where the slippery slope, or slow road begins... God, the Universe or whatever you believe. Some might call this being open minded and accepting, sure, but it's a risky position when you know the Word and I'm not willing to make that interpretation considering what has been directly said by Jesus. In his most important preaching, the Sermon on the Mount, Jesus said *Many will say to Me in that day (judgment day), 'Lord, Lord, have we not prophesied in Your name, cast out demons in Your name, and done many wonders in Your name?' And then I will declare to them, 'I never knew you; depart from Me, you who practice lawlessness!'*

Harmless or costly? Some will argue, because the god (small g) has made a big impact on their life, harmless. To which I understand, but it's costly at the risk that your identity in Christ is superseded by an identity in a false idol. Remember Aeschylus said *"It is easy when we are in prosperity to give advice to the afflicted."* Desperate people often pay large sums of money they can't afford to hear the wisdom of a small god on stage and then are asked to pay extra for a photo opportunity with them. I know because I've done it. It's a fine line right? Nothing is wrong with taking a photo with somebody you admire, but charging for it defines it as idolatry and it's not just a financial risk but a spiritual one.

Exodus, Deuteronomy, Joshua, Psalms and Corinthians all clearly state that idolatry is a severe offense and the first of the Ten Commandments is "You shall have no other gods before me." It's not first by coincidence. We place things which are most important first, need anything more be said?

It's so subtle, so cleverly cloaked in the manipulation of words and such a nuance to some, that I'm not surprised most people casually overlook it. Again, it's not my job to reprimand you, it's my goal to lead you to the foundational truth so you can make a decision for yourself. Angelike and I have come to an agreement that we must audit the use of our language and beliefs systems as to what we will or will not tolerate in accordance with the Word of God, because Jesus said, there will be many who have a form of godliness, but none thereof. Demons are capable of providing material benefits so we have to be highly discerning and wise to the fact that power and the desire to be powerful often come cloaked in a form of godliness.

You'll recall early on we defined follower as, *to accept as authority; to be or act in accordance with.* Who has dominion, or influence, over us? If an earthly teacher or authority I follow can subvert my attention away from God's law, then I've given dominion to a false idol. It serves to repeat, as my knowledge of God's Word increased, I found myself on several occasions having to walk out of self development seminars where I felt other spirits, demonic spirits, were allowed access to the room. If you're an agnostic or new to Christianity, this may seem childish or supercilious. But if you're mature in the Word, then you know why.

So why does it matter?

I FIGHT AUTHORITY,
AUTHORITY ALWAYS WINS

As a journalist of 25 years and business coach of ten, I've interviewed thousands of people and have asked tens of thousands of questions. In journalism it's known as the 5 Ws; who, what, when, where and why. Who said it? What does it mean? When did it happen? Where did it come from? Why is it true or does it matter?

The next very common sense question for you is from what book or by what authority does the Universe speak? Does Mother Nature have a nature to her heart? Have either claimed to have written anything, penned moral laws or spoken to human beings?

The problem isn't with the idea that there is indeed power in nature, and our universe as a whole, the problem is we are crediting the creation, not the Creator.

The heavens declare the glory of God;
the skies proclaim the work of his hands.
(Psalm 19:1)

Can any of these methods or belief systems lay claim to why or how? It's that simple, there is either a source or there isn't. You can't explain something by saying, "just because," remember? I recall one guy in the Secret saying he asks for a parking space and one opens up, or he begins to manifest money and checks start magically appealing in the mail. He gives no rhyme or reason as to how, but says just because he focused on it. Maybe it is something supernatural that opens up the parking space or puts money in our lap and if that's the direction some go in, then it brings us to the next question. If it's not God, then it must be a counterfeit of him.

The Bible is very clear that there is a supernatural world. But where we get things confused or mixed up is when we play around with the supernatural and don't call on THE HOLY SPIRIT but instead leave the door wide open for other spirits. Jesus said *"Most assuredly, I say to you, the man who does not enter the sheep pen gate, but climbs in some other way, is a thief and a robber."* John 10:1

We have a loving but jealous God, and when we mess around with the supernatural apart from Him, and credit that which mocks His authority, then we enter into territory that has no boundaries.

IT MATTERS

Authorship is important. If I put other people's words in this book and claimed them as my own without giving them credit, is that ethical? No, that's why there are copyright laws. In the business world people are awarded patents and trademarks and everybody seems to understand this. So when the words, ideas, blessings and love of the Almighty God are stolen, plagiarized or bereft of his authority or signature, is it not the same?

It matters to God and that's not my opinion, but something stated on several occasions in scripture. The Word is very clear in telling us that God is a jealous God and that we are not to bow down or serve false idols.

This topic of God vs. The Universe is contentious in today's world because many are trying to appease and gain followers and at the end, can they say yes, God I believed in you; but I also called you the Universe, but I didn't really mean it. Will this ignorance be ok to God? He knows your heart but what do your actions say - do they match up with that. Is that a gamble you want to take?

I'll ask you again, why is it the first commandment? For a reason; You shall not have strange Gods before me…You shall not adore them nor serve them. By name they are called false idols because they are not the same as the God of Israel, the God of Moses and the God of Abraham. One has a lengthy, well established history of fulfilled prophecies, eye witnesses and secular historians of antiquity to back it up. But what about the others? The others just are? And those who like to say "the Bible, but this too" or "whatever you believe" clearly don't understand the Word, and what it says a jealous God means.

DO YOU REALLY WANT TO HURT ME

God's nature is always up for a heated debate by those who have been what's called "church hurt," which is clearly understandable. Angelike and I are highly sympathetic to those who have been hurt, either physically or mentally, by religion. But that's man, using free will while under the control of the devil and using religion to inflict pain. It's not God. And it's a very good reason for people to turn their attention to other things.

Understandably, the term jealous God is, in and of itself, an easy target for some of those who subscribe to the Universe or other similar new age beliefs to further attack God or negate his word. However, I believe it also presents a unique opportunity to do quite the opposite, by putting God's character and benevolence to the test. To illustrate this point, someone could say something like how can such a loving God be jealous? Jealousy isn't good. As long as you're a good person, it shouldn't matter by what name you call God.

But the name you call God by does matter, and the answer as to why should appeal to any person's common sense. The proper response is that we should absolutely, one hundred percent, prefer a jealous God because then we know he's a relational God and we know that we matter to him. If he weren't described as jealous, I'd be worried, I'd be skeptical of his Word. It's much the same way as if my wife said she loves me but didn't care if I saw other women. I'd question her love for me. I want her to be jealous in that manner. It's a healthy jealousy. Just like Jesus called us by name, because he is relational and we are his.

Let's take it one step further and maybe this will help. Imagine for a second you take your child to the park one day. He is playing with other children and having a good time. Another parent approaches you and compliments your child saying "wow, how well behaved your son is." But before you can open your mouth, the stranger on the park bench seated next to you says "thank you, I appreciate that." Would that sit well with you? You're a nice person after all, so why should it matter? Who cares who gets credit? All that should matter is that he is a nice boy. But of course it matters. What if the stranger said "well, we both can take credit for him, right?" You'd say that child is the fruit of my labor, I made him, gave him my love, my tutelage. I sacrificed for him. Who are you to take credit for it?

By choosing to leave out the author of life, the one who gave us our breath, we are only using a counterfeit tool of the Devil, but it's deception at its finest. Does it produce some results? Perhaps. But so does black magic.

Watch constantly against those things which are thought to be no temptations. The most poisonous serpents are found where the sweetest flowers grow. Cleopatra was poisoned by an asp that was brought to her in a basket of fair flowers.
- Charles Spurgeon

I WANNA GET NEXT TO YOU

If we're being transparent, we have to place some of the blame on religion. Organized religion slowly became a mechanism for man to control man rather than man to evangelize and teach man. It became more about a governing authority and control and less about the carrying on of Biblical doctrine and God's Word. It's why Luther confronted the Church in 1517 and began the Protestant Reformation. God's Word became tainted, fractured and distorted in a way that imprisoned people more than it freed them. It's why many people are what I mentioned as being "church hurt."

I find it so paradoxical today that our culture can fund a movie franchise like the Avengers, we can believe in karma, put crystals around our necks and tune into every conceivable evil on the news each night, but the concept of a loving a *supernatural* God is far fetched to some people?

If people are feeling "left out" and "left searching" it's because the Church is "leaving out" the most wonderful and dynamic parts of the Word. This is where I really sympathize with non-believers, the people walking around thirsting to know a big God, craving the knowledge and power of a supernatural God but aren't being told about Him because the Word is being watered down, because some Christian religions leave out the supernatural or teach that it only existed in Biblical times.

By neglecting to teach the most awesome and supernatural parts of the Bible, by putting miracles in the past and not the present, we, the Church, are doing God a disservice. The Bible absent of the supernatural leaves Christianity as just another belief system. I say don't give me bits and pieces, the ritual and recital, I want the awe-inspiring supernatural character of God to be known. I feel this is why so many stray and find themselves playing around with mediums, necromancers and dangerous "spiritual" entities, because by not teaching the supernatural, then the vacuum we leave will be filled by the devil, false idols cloaked in a lie.

To be clear, this doesn't mean that to be a believer it should require the high of miraculous experience to justify their connection with God, let's not exaggerate. It's just that in a world begging for meaning and direction, so many are left to linger in doubt, walking about in quiet desperation, self medicating on anything else that gives them a sense of temporary direction or confidence. There is an abundance of spiritually thirsty people, who don't know they've been chosen, who don't know that the supernatural God of the Bible is alive and well and doing things every day that would amaze them. These same people are then gravitating toward organizations and communities absent of the Word because their feelings of loneliness or lack of self worth are being quenched by some type of psuedogod rather than foundational truth.

I'M FREE TO DO WHAT I WANT ANY OLD TIME

Another allure of these counterfeit gods is fairly obvious and rather easy to understand, and that's accountability. Our culture thrives on not being responsible for our own actions and pursuing a lust for life over the pursuit of righteousness, so who wouldn't want all the benefits of a supernatural belief system without having to be obedient to God and his laws? If I offered my daughter a credit card, with no limitations on her spending, no rules for using the card by way of behaving, doing chores or acting in accordance with my house rules, is that a belief system or a one way street?

Paul foretold this, saying there would be a time when people would turn from the Word and lust after teachers who told them what they wanted to hear. In other words, give me the version of a God that is full of abundance and pleasure yet devoid of any moralities which are inconvenient to my lifestyle. He said people would have "itching ears" and turn to fables. Exactly, and the second part of every fable is what? It's that somebody or something is hiding something from you.

Our world is in a moral nosedive, a downward plunge. Who benefits by not telling you about God's laws and His goodness? Who benefits most by a culture in constant chaos and immorality? I'm sure you can come up with an answer.

I know these paragraphs can seem a bit "preachy" but I assure you, my desire is for God's true Word, not religion, to be uncovered *or* revealed to you so that you can give life to all those plans you have for success and author something bigger than you ever imagined. God doesn't exist in fairy tales or fables, he isn't hiding anything from you. He's real and right in front of you.

Let him build.

When you build a house (i.e. your faith) on things which are temporal, it will be weak and you will end up looking for mechanisms to support to it, which is why things such as Strengthfinders, Enneagrams and color codes have gained such popularity over the last couple of decades. They serve to prop up a fragile construction given by gods (small g) because they satisfy our human desire of validation. Tell me who I already think I am and tell me what I am not and that way I can stay in my comfort zone. Tell me what I'm capable of and what I shouldn't try so I don't go outside of the limits of the world.

These things aren't terrible, I'm guilty of using them in the past, but we can't allow them to become our identity and confirm what we perceive as our limitations. Imagine what would have happened had Noah or Moses or Mary been subject to them. Noah, you're a number three; pragmatic and image-Conscious. Moses, you're a Nine, a peacemaker, easy going and complacent. Mary, you're a One, a rational, perfectionist.

My purpose is not to cast judgment on those who subscribe to these things but rather have them rationally look at what it means to be categorized by them. Weigh what they say who you are versus what God, who says all things are possible through me, says you are.

It's a simple question of dominion and what you give power to. Are you looking more to a strengthsfinder or enneagram number to guide you? Or despite the "findings" and interpretations of that, are you standing on the Word of God to say, no matter what *that* says, I am the temple of the Holy Spirit and all things are possible through Him, what *HE* says about my life, and walk boldly in that wisdom?

I'm aware that these things are very close to people's hearts and entire belief systems are built upon them. We can agree to disagree and I'm not the ultimate judge of what is right or wrong. My desire is that this resonates enough for you to ask questions and dig deeper. All of the subject matter in this chapter has been around hot button topics, but the stakes are too high not to bring them up. To be here on this earth for 70 or so years and not have God's Word is tough. What's tougher is not having hope or knowledge of what's next. None of those other sources give any mention as to what happens to your soul after your days here are up. Nothing is written on this by them on the subject. However God's Word addresses it very clearly.

IT'S NOT YOU IT'S ME

It's the oldest line in dating and it's so overused that nobody believes it when they hear it, *it's not you it's me*. People say it when they're avoiding a relationship that's difficult or uncomfortable and want an easy way out minus the burden of guilt. But who are we kidding? Nobody on either side of the relationship buys it and the same goes for a spiritual relationship. We can't fool God any more than we can fool ourselves. As clever as we think we are, He knows our heart, so maybe it's time to be honest and have a real heart to heart talk with Him.

The other big lie we all say along the course of a romantic relationship is "I don't like playing games." It's on every dating profile, *I'm a straight shooter, no games please,* but in case you haven't noticed, the ones who repeat that line most often are what, yup, the ones who play the most games.

During the most critical times of my life, when I thought I was being honest in my spiritual relationship with God, I wasn't at all. I treated Him kinda like DoorDash - thinking I could just place my order to fill my belly and then wait on Him to deliver it to my porch. When that didn't happen, it was His fault, not mine. I placed blame on Him, not myself, because I was taking the *quid pro quo* approach. Ok God, if I do this, then you'll do that. Sometimes we wish it worked that way, but it doesn't.

Somehow, he finally broke through to me. He always has a way of reaching the most reluctant people. Why? Because truth permeates places where walls have been constructed to keep it out and people have been persuaded to speak against it.

It permeates the slightest cracks and whispers in the ears of those too afraid to admit they seek it. That's how it found me, but I'll admit, I needed a little bit more, I needed hard evidence, as blind faith was not my gift. That's why I included the *Did You Know* sections at the end of each chapter. To give evidence for those who need it.

The day in, day out onslaughts of manufactured cultural crises and embellished idols have managed to accomplish exactly what the enemy wanted, to keep people from focusing on the foundational wisdom of God's word. It's all a giant distraction.

We sit in anticipation, waiting for direction from influencers and politicians to give us their take, their philosophy, but they've only been building blocks of massive change away from the foundational principles of creation. It's God's philosophy, his building blocks that have changed so many millions of lives over the centuries.

Speaking from personal experience, for years I was led to believe that the God of the Bible wasn't relevant to my current problems and frustrations and therefore gave myself permission to doubt and believe I wasn't qualified to receive anything good. Thoughts like, what if I offended God in my past? What if I'm not good enough for him? Who am I to think I can be chosen? They are all words we choose to focus on, those are not His words.

My goal is not to point fingers or mock anybody for their belief system but rather to ask a very common sense question, if your belief system has no foundation, how can you trust it? Just because?

Now that you know the invitation is there and you are chosen by God, it's time to choose back and truly begin *The Pursuit*.

DID YOU KNOW?

Did you know that the Bible clearly addresses and defines concepts of how the earth was created, love, marriage, politeness and where we go after we die.

When you put the Bible up against other belief systems, you must ask these questions:

Does the universe describe how it came into being?

> *And God said, "Let there be light," and there was light."*
> *Genesis 1:3*

Does it say how man was made?

> *Then the LORD God formed a man from the dust of*
> *the ground and breathed into his nostrils the breath of life,*
> *and the man became a living being.*
> *Genesis 2:7*

Does it say why we look the way we look?

> *So God created man in his own image, in the image of God*
> *he created him; male and female he created them*
> *Genesis 1:27*

Does the universe define love?

> *Love is patient, love is kind. It does not envy, it does not boast*
> *1 Corinthians 13:4*

How does it define marriage?

*Therefore a man shall leave his father and his mother
and hold fast to his wife, and they shall become one flesh*
Gen. 2:24

What does it say about how we should treat one another?

"Be kind and compassionate." Eph 4:32,

"Encourage one another and build one another up"
1 Thessalonians 5:11

Does it say how long we will live or where we will go after we die?

His days shall be one hundred and twenty years Gen. 6:3

My Father's house has many rooms.
And I will prepare a place for you. John 14

When we look at the Word of God, it's very specific in regards to all of these things. It answers all of our deepest questions about life in the kind of rich detail that only a supernatural document can do.

CHAPTER 8

HANGIN' TOUGH

For we do not wrestle against flesh and blood, but against the rulers,
against the authorities, against the cosmic powers over this present
darkness, against the spiritual forces of evil in the heavenly places.
- Ephesians 6: 12-18

There I sat one Sunday early in 2021, watching our church service online in my living room. That's when I heard it, that familiar promise - Jeremiah 29:11, which says God has plans to prosper me and give me hope for a good future.

That's great I thought, but when? My family and I were tired of waiting so all I heard was "Prosperity party of five, your table is ready" and I was like Yea, Ok, that's us, let's do this.

It was also at that moment when curiosity got the best of me and I decided to do a little digging into the book of Jeremiah to see if I could get clear on what this wonderful sounding scripture really meant. What followed was a timely message that completely changed my perspective on the verse.

In the context of this scripture, the prophet Jeremiah is speaking to the people of Israel who had become extremely lazy in their ways. They went on cruise control having been spoiled with good times and slowly, over time, came to the conclusion that they really didn't have a need for God's laws or instruction any longer. So they began worshiping false idols and making sacrifices to other gods. They did wicked things and turned their backs on the good fortune God had bestowed upon them. What's significant for us, living now in the present, is that the people of Israel ignored the repeated warnings they were given by Jeremiah who was literally begging them to change their ways and straighten out. I was amazed to learn that nearly the entire book of Jeremiah is him warning the people over and over and over again to get their act together or else. Specifically he told them if they didn't straighten up and correct their wicked ways that invaders would come from the north and take over their land. Even worse, they would be exiled and enslaved to their enemy, King Nebuchadnezzar of Babylon.

Warnings should be taken seriously, because as journalist Norman Cousins once put it, **history is a vast early warning system.** And here we are, getting ready to put God's Word and history to the test again. Proud and ambitious men and women continue to ignore the lessons of the past and once thriving countries and cities have become places of Godlessness.

BAD MOON RISING

When Jeremiah receives his instructions from God, telling the people of Israel that they will prosper, it's exactly what the Jewish people want to hear. They regret not heeding his initial warning but at least they won't suffer long. Can you picture what that would look like today, where somebody steps up and says: the pandemic is over, the economy will thrive, the left and the right will join together in the middle and life as we know it will go back to normal. Therefore marry, have babies and be happy.

You'd be on board with that, perhaps thinking "Yup, we should've done a better job listening to God first but I'm ready for full normalcy again." Normal, which we took for granted, is nice isn't it?

But now imagine that person saying "well, there's one caveat, we've got 70 more years of pandemic, oppression and political polarization and war, but then it gets better."

"Excuse me, did you just say 70 more years? Well that stinks. That's not what I wanted to hear." I can tell you this, it's not what the Jewish people wanted to hear either. NOW, is more along the lines of what they were thinking. NOW would be a great time to restore our lives to normal. As I said earlier, time is always a factor in God's teachings and it is one of the things we, as human beings, have a hard time processing, but in scripture, where it matters most, it is very specific in the stories and teachings.

Now is also a good time to get a clearer, more accurate definition, or in this case translation, of the word prosperity as it was written in the original Hebrew text of Jeremiah 29:11. The word was Tsalach {tsaw-lakh'}. It is used 66 times in the Bible and it is most often translated to "prosper" in English but has many definitions such as **be good, break out, come mightily and be profitable.** But I would like to bring to your attention a more accurate translation for this particular time in our lives and why Jeremiah 29:11 is so significant to us now - that is **"to push forward."**

Prosperity (Tsalach) in this context means to push forward in or into God's promises. Yes, we can be profitable in our bank accounts but first we must seek to be profitable in the spirit. It's not unlike how you were rewarded by your earthly father. There were times when you were expected to do something and you received a reward or allowance in terms of money. But I'm sure you can recall other times when your father taught you a lesson in virtue and patience, and looking back it was of much greater value than if he had handed you a dollar.

I have a very hard working and virtuous daughter who loves to get prospered in the form of cash from Dad. However she also likes to test her boundaries and on occasion gets a bit too rebellious for her own good. It's in those times that I give her the type of prosperity that comes in the form of a life lesson, and it always involves a moral lesson that will pay off in the future.

Not surprisingly, she's not as big of a fan of those rewards right now, but what type of parent would I be without unconditional love as a foundational promise between me and my daughter? And what type of parent would I be without discipline and correction as a foundational obligation between her and I as well?

The value in discovering the Word is that it lets us know that we are loved and important. The value in continuing to read it is that it reminds us how to get healed when we are broken, set on the path when we drift off course. In our physical body, when we have a cut, what happens? We're hardwired to mend and restore. You don't have to start that healing process, there is no button to push that says, stop bleeding and scab up, God designed us to repair. The same can be said for instances in which we cut ourselves spiritually. We have a built in mechanism for healing, it's called prayer of intercession. There's no prerequisite for it, you don't have to physically do anything yourself, you just hit your knees and surrender to His grace.

Tsalach means we have the capability to push forward and have hope even when it seems as if there is little. It means that God has a plan to heal us when the emotional bleeding starts and we feel like quitting. It's not the monetary prosperity we're in need of most during these times, it's the confidence to know that no matter the situation, we're not alone in the fight. Furthermore, tsalach directly relates to the most critical and repeated message of Jesus Christ's ministry while here on earth, and that is the message of hope.

HOMEWARD BOUND

To be exiled means a period of forced or voluntary absence. The Jewish people of Jeremiah's time were forced into Babylon, we on the other hand, in our modern world, have taken more of a voluntary path. We've willingly been led away from a life we've known to either a small, or sometimes a large, degree. In physical terms, yes, we're still in America but spiritually, relative to the life we've known, we're far removed from the world many of us grew up in. We are now desperately looking for a renewed sense of hope.

For decades, we've given free reign to our leaders who've spent too much, fought too much and have gotten fat off the land. As individuals, we've also regressed, willingly going against positions of morality when we are hard pressed to get ahead. Little by little, the laws of the Bible are being circumvented, culture is saying it's fine without God leading the way.

What does it all add up to? Deception, coercion and a hiding of the truth.

In The Matrix movie, did anybody look at Neo when he realized he was in a make believe, artificial reality and say, yea, that looks like a promising future and a means to achieve happiness so let's continue to go in that direction? No, Neo was oblivious to his situation because he was under the deception of those pulling the strings.

Remember when I said earlier that most people think the problem is too big for lil'old me, and what did I say in response? No, we fix ourselves and that is how we fix the world. What's that look like? It begins with opening our eyes and decreasing the overwhelm and distraction in our own lives. In my house, we see the pop star Billie Eilish, who looks like Linda Blair in the Exorcist on her album cover and who is now being drawn as a Disney Princess and see that this is like the false idol that scripture warned us about.

Think about all the different positions of authority in our world. Everybody was so worried about who the President was that we blinded ourselves to who really had the most impact over our daily lives, City Halls and School Boards. That was a huge wake up call.

As for the big guns, the "democratically elected" men and women of the United States Congress, you can go to their Wikipedia pages and read about their *Early Life* and *Education*, it's all there in black and white. Despite their continuous assurance of a belief in God and their often parochial educations, they still insist on legislating in favor of things which directly contradict God's Word. They build in the same vein that King Nebuchadnezzar of Babylon built, by turning the people away from wisdom and towards more division and more war. Common sense question; who benefits from wars and violence? The people or their rulers?

Take notice that in no way is this book a sad story. But I can't tell you about the victory and the prosperity to come if I don't first point out the obvious, that indeed we too have been given over as captives exactly as the Israelites were. We're prisoners of a different sort, unknowingly deceived by wolves in sheeps clothing. The Bible says that people would **depart from the faith by devoting themselves to deceitful spirits and teachings of demons**. It's happening little by little.

It's hard to say exactly what stage of Jeremiah we mirror most, but to think we're not down to our last warning would be naive. Up until recently, things in the world were good and the majority of people felt safe, nothing life (style) threatening was happening, certainly nothing catastrophic. We all began to nestle up by the warm fireplace, checking our status updates and waiting for DoorDash as the kids sat on their devices, somewhere in the house, following somebody too. How could that possibly go bad, I ask with a high degree of sarcasm.

Hear my words, victory is coming. Triumph is near, but only when we wake up to the fact that comfort is the enemy of progress, and getting real comfortable is an invitation for calamity.

PRODIGAL SON

For a second, let's revisit the image of the rebellious teenager. How many of us packed our bag one frustrated evening and told ourselves we were running away from home and that we didn't need our parents stupid rules. We didn't need their love. We thought things would be much better if they just left us alone. We said *They're so old, they have no idea what I'm going through.*

The parallels between our earthly and heavenly father cannot be understated. Our world at the present moment is that rebellious teen and we've reached the point where maybe we don't need to pay attention to that ancient book. How could it possibly be of much use to us now, you know it being so old and us being so young and evolved. We don't need no stupid rules. We make our own decisions.

Yea, that's also a heavy dose of sarcasm, but even for myself, somebody who has always grown up with faith, I was captured by the allure of a culture which drew me away from God to the point where he didn't play a central role in my life. I certainly didn't see a need to co-create with him because the gods (small g) had taken center stage, they were the ones popping up on my smartphone every day offering all I needed to know in terms of money, sex and success.

Now that pestilence and division are central figures in our daily lives, for the first time most of us can acknowledge that our foundation is shaky. A lot of people are curious about what's in that "old book" they call the Bible, asking themselves what do so many people respect and appreciate it for?

It's hard to ignore the awakening taking place, the lukewarm believers, those whose Bibles may have been collecting dust on a shelf somewhere, have been ignited, and suddenly these once taboo topics of faith and salvation are popping up amongst friends on text threads and during family get-togethers. It's even prevalent on our social media feeds (when it's not being censored out) as people are asking *can't we just get back to normal, please.*

I don't know when or how, but what I am here to tell you is that we will tsalach (push forward) and I believe we still have an opportunity to turn things around because we serve a loving and forgiving God who never relents in his pursuit of our hearts.

Like the prodigal son, the father is waiting at home with open arms for those ready to return home and embrace Him. The Word describes the Kingdom of Heaven like a wedding banquet, some come and some refuse the invitation as we cannot forget free will. Will you ignore the invitation and put more distance between yourself and home or will you join The Pursuit and seek a relationship with your heavenly father?

A POWER STRUGGLE

The parallels between Jeremiah and our current situation go deep. During Jeremiah's time there were other prophets, false prophets, who were going around prophesying an immediate fix, telling the people it was going to get better right now. If you recall during the rather tumultuous time period leading up to the 2020 election we heard about similar prophecies which told of an uncovering of the enemy.

We were told by modern day prophets of social media that a justice from the Lord and a freeing of His people from the tyrannical forces of evil was imminent.

This was a particular feeling expressed in the Qanon movement, which often alluded to a day of reckoning approaching from a supernatural source. A higher power was playing 4-D chess and soon freedom would come and wrongs would be righted. Each new deadline came and went though. The sure signs were not so sure after all. But what does the Bible say is the true test of a prophet?

If what a prophet proclaims in the name of the Lord does not take place or come true, that is a message the Lord has not spoken.
Deuteronomy 18:22 reads

To say we have to be alert in the spirit is an understatement. We need to pray for the gift of discernment to manifest itself to the highest degree inside of us, asking ourselves, what is God's word and what is a manipulation of it. This will be critical in the coming years. False teaching and false prophecy will pop up over and over again and we must be equally patient and diligent because the fact is, we don't know God's timing. His time to act will come and until then, like so many times in previous Biblical history, there is an excruciating ebb and flow between despair and optimism amongst believers, but remember, we are called to rise above it, as *We know that we are children of God, and that the whole world is under the control of the evil one* (1 John 5:19) and *Judgment will come because the ruler of this world has already been judged* (John 16:11).

Habakkuk was a prophet of the Bible who lived roughly 600 years before Jesus Christ. During his time, he was pained at what he witnessed, lawlessness and a complete resistance to morality. This was his complaint:

"How long, Lord, must I call for help, but you do not listen? Or cry out to you, 'Violence!' but you do not save? Why do you make me look at injustice? Why do you tolerate wrongdoing? Destruction and violence are before me; there is strife, and conflict abounds. Therefore the law is paralysed, and justice never prevails. The wicked hem in the righteous, so that justice is perverted."

Can you imagine what Habakkuk would've done had he had access to Twitter? Although I joke, it's not funny because so many people feel exactly like him these days. We cry out for help and become frustrated when our demands are not immediately met.

Before we shake another fist or go on another rant, let's learn the lesson of prosperity we're supposed to get from Jeremiah. Repent and do what's right. God's patience and His promises are not a big secret, but there is a reluctance of many to ignore them. Jeremiah tells of a drifting and a course correction, a turning away followed by an intercession. This is where we can all do something to save what we love. Revive the Word.

Time after time we see men and women of the Bible who prayed and pleaded with the Lord to be merciful and give their culture one more chance to course correct, while at the same time, their desire was to help man avoid stepping in the path of his own destruction, speaking to the people about the desires of the Father. Be one of those people, speak to God and man to help bring them together.

I remind you, people can attempt to drill into your head what to think, what to say and how to act but they can't touch your spirit when you are in alignment with God. We're never not in control of our own thoughts. In all circumstances throughout history in which man has betrayed the original instructions in regard to God's word, there was first a naivety to be misinformed followed by a willingness to align with misbehave.

Free will. It's critical for every believer to understand the significance of it.

Please know this, what follows from this moment on is more important than anything that's happened until now in your life. Jeremiah 29:12 is just as, if not more important, than what came before it in 29:11 because it says, "**You will call on me and come to pray to me, and I will listen to you. You will seek me and find me when you seek me with all your heart.**"

What can we glean from scripture? I believe it says that we have work to do on our end. We must be *in pursuit*. We must accept the invitation and take direction. We don't need to reimagine or reset, we need to revive. Revive the Word of God and thus the world shall be revived and be brought back to life.

WE DON'T NEED NO CIVIL WAR

Look at the hate we're breeding
Look at the fear we're feeding
Look at the lives we're leading
The way we've always done before

There's an old Paul Newman film titled Cool Hand Luke and the most famous line from it, which perhaps you've heard, goes like this; **What we have here is a failure to communicate.** If you don't go back that far, you might recall it being the sound bite to open Guns N' Roses song *Civil War*. Read the lyrics above again and tell me they're not applicable to what we see these days. Again, humanity is in rebellion against God and His desire is to restore the relationship.

From my perspective, as the author of this book, this is where I get really excited for you, because I was you. I was rebelling like crazy and God was down to His last chance with me, which I say humbly and lovingly. Like a human father, he taught me about who makes the rules while at the same time leaving the door open for my return. We as a people and a nation are the prodigal sons. The father is at home, waiting for us, ready to welcome us with open arms upon our return. No questions. No blaming. Just acceptance. When that happens, the world changes.

Remember Habbakuk? The Lord answered his complaint saying **'Look at the nations and watch – and be utterly amazed. For I am going to do something in your days that you would not believe, even if you were told."**

We, as individuals must fix ourselves in order to fix the world. Go ahead, be open to seeking him. Because it isn't that God doesn't have plans for you, there's just been a failure to communicate and nobody explained to you how powerful His word is.

DID YOU KNOW?

The Torah (first 5 books of the Bible) has 304,805 letters and 79,976 words in Hebrew. Each manuscript or copy was meticulously written by Jewish scholars and any inconsistencies in the copies were thrown away. No other literature in history comes close to the accuracy of the Jewish Scriptures.

- No word or even a letter could be written from memory. A scribe must have another scroll open before him and pronounce every word out loud before copying it.
- Before writing the name of God, a scribe must reverently wipe his pen and say, "I am writing the name of God for the holiness of His name."
- Every letter had to have some space around it. If one letter touched another or if a letter was defective because of incorrect writing, a hole, a tear, or a smudge so that it could not be easily read, the scroll was invalidated.
- Within thirty days of completion, an editor would review the manuscript, count every letter and every word as a way of checking. The editor would also make sure that the middle word on each page of the copy was the same as the middle words on the manuscript being copied. (Ref: StoryoftheBible. com)

Any minor inconsistencies that people speak of are along the lines of something like *Went to Jerusalem* vs. *Went up to Jerusalem*

The Hebrew language has not changed in thousands of years, meaning anybody who can read Hebrew today can look at the ancient text of the Torah and read it with nearly 100 percent accuracy.

One scholar said that it is like asking a modern Egyptian to walk into a Pyramid and read hieroglyphics.

I pulled up a letter from a soldier in the Civil War and asked my daughter to read it and that was difficult. Imagine, that was only 157 years ago.

The point is that no other language has been so meticulously clean as to record and save history with complete accuracy than that of the Hebrew language.

RD Wilson was an American linguist and Old Testament Scholar of the early 20th century. In his book *A Scientific Investigation into the Old Testament,* he writes:

The names of these kings – about forty in all – are the names of men who lived from about 2000 to 400 B.C. and yet they each and all appear in proper chronological order both with reference to the kings of the same country and with respect to the kings of other countries contemporary with them. No stronger evidence for the substantial accuracy of the Old Testament records could possibly be imagined than this collection of names of kings.

CHAPTER 9

A SIMPLE PLAN

*"We must make a study of our God: what He loves, what He hates,
how He speaks and acts. We cannot imitate a God whose
features and habits we have never learned"*
- Jen Wilkin

In the fall of 1973, a little southern rock band from Jacksonville, Florida released their debut album. The fourth song on that record was a homage to the lead singer's grandmother and the guitarist's mother and the words of wisdom those women shared with their boys before their passing.

The women gave a common sense list of advice they felt would serve the young men as they got older. They warned them not to do anything too crazy and that they would be well served by finding somebody to love. They told them not to just chase money but rather seek fulfillment in their work, to do something that agrees with their soul. They predicted that there would be hard times in life but reassured the boys not to let those hard times get them down, that they would eventually pass. One more thing mama said, she said don't forget, son, there is someone up above.

The song was called *Simple Man,* by Lynard Skynard, and were it not for a little number called *Sweet Home Alabama* and something called *Free Bird* it might've been the star of the album. It's an appropriate introduction to this chapter as what you're about to find out is that the best advice is simple advice and if there is one thing modern man has definitely mastered, it's confusion.

Confusion and impotence are the inevitable results when the
wisdom and resources of the world are substituted
for the presence and power of the Spirit.
- Samuel Chadwick

Man has complicated the uncomplicated. For instance, House Bill H.R. 5376, submitted to the 117th Congress on September 27, 2021, which is better known as the Build Back Better bill, is 2,468 pages. Trying to find out who has actually read it is only trumped by attempting to find out who actually authored it.

God tells us to simply give 10 percent of our income to helping others. The Internal Revenue Service calls for seven different tax brackets and a staff of nearly 75,000.

God made two genders, man and woman. Culture has attempted to identify over 70 different genders.

God gave us the Ten Commandments. Man has created a book of laws that would stack higher than the Tower of Babel.

But perhaps the most tragic of all things man has complicated is the Church, which has to take some accountability for taking a simple plan and chopping it up into 200 different belief systems. Some call it a collision between Christ and culture and others believe it to be a straight up rebellion. Regardless, it comes down to one simple fact: Jesus was neither a Baptist, a Lutheran, a Methodist, a Episcopalian or a Pentacostal. In fact, he was never called a Christian. He was born a Jew and died a Jew and He came to redeem the world, not to complicate it. With that in mind, let's establish one simple rule that Jesus came to reinforce: ***above all others, Love the Lord your God with all your heart and with all your soul and with all your mind*** and when you get that clear, proceed to rule No. 2, **love your neighbor as yourself.** Two commands. That's simple right? The first is, but that second one isn't as easy as we'd like it to be these days. I'll repeat the Tozer quote; *I believe you can be right with God and still not like the way some people behave.* We can still love without condoning, it's that simple.

As we've ignored the divine order once more, and history seems to be repeating itself yet again, we again have to ask ourselves some simple questions about our future.

Does freedom still ring?

Who is in charge?

Does the Lord still have plans to prosper me and give me hope for a future?

When it comes to answering those questions, one has to go back to dominion and authority? Throughout history, when man has encroached upon God's dominion and authority, what's followed has always been an abuse of power and human rights. Instead of loving one's neighbor, man seeks to control their neighbor. Our greatest weapon in avoiding this mistake again is to teach wisdom. For where we find wisdom, we also find liberty. No greater is the foundational wisdom of scripture. It has passed the test of time. It's why the Bible still sits as king on the all-time bestsellers list with about 5 billion copies in print. To put that number in perspective, look at the numbers from the Quran (800 million) and the Book of Mormon (120 million). As one pastor so eloquently put it, the Bible is timeless and therefore it is timely. Its wisdom transcends time and culture and in the hand of the righteous, is the ultimate weapon in any war of words.

We need only to go back to the great abolitionist Frederick Douglas who said *Knowledge makes a man unfit to be a slave.* Not surprising because Douglas was a preacher and that statement is in direct relation to what Jesus says in John's Gospel, "*the truth will set you free.*" It's precisely what lent the inspiration to the subtitle of this book.

Whose truth? As I said in chapter one, these days we're asked to accept everybody's truth, but the truth really has just one author. The truth that will set you free comes from Jesus, who says it is "my teaching." So if it's simple and it's the truth, why are we straying from it? Let's take a revival course and see.

3 SIMPLE STEPS

If you look just one track above Simple Man on that same Lynard Skynard album, you'll find the song *Gimmie Three Steps*. It's about a man who's gotten into a bar fight and is fearing for his life, asking the guy he's in an argument with if he can have a three step head start to run for the door. It's a typical southern rock song you might say. But let's run it alongside what's happening in our world today. We're in a bit of a confrontation of our own here, the devil has started a scuffle. We can run or we can fight. I'm about to give you three steps, but not toward the exit, but toward the fight.

STEP 1: GET WISDOM

At this moment in history, the same Biblical wisdom that's been available to all generations is trying to be hidden from you. We see prayer being taken out of schools and the Ten Commandments taken out of government buildings. Men of the cloth are even taking Biblical doctrine out of the church. But that's nothing new, God's law has always been under assault, even by those who claimed it as their own. As Christians, we're told where there is no vision, the people perish. Well, it's hard to have vision without wisdom and it's hard to have wisdom if you are forbidden access to it.

We prohibit laymen possessing copies of the Old and New Testament...
We forbid them most severely to have the above books in the popular
vernacular. . . . The lords of the districts shall carefully seek out the
heretics in dwellings, hovels, and forests, and even their
underground retreats shall be entirely wiped out.
- Pope Gregory IX, Council. Tolosanum, Anno. Chr. 1229

Foundational wisdom is meant to be imparted by parents onto their children as we see in the following verses:

(Proverbs 22:6) Train up a child in the way he should go; even when he is old he will not depart from it.

(Ephesians 6:4) Fathers, but bring them up in the discipline and instruction of the Lord.

(Deuteronomy 6:7) You shall teach them laws diligently to your children, and shall talk of them when you sit in your house, and when you walk by the way, and when you lie down, and when you rise.

But when longstanding institutions such as the home and the church have cracks in them, there is a scattering of the truth, a wandering of the people, and when we wander, we open ourselves up to temptation and deception. When secondary foundations such as schools and governments also have cracks and become complicit in hiding the truth, then we see what's happening right now, a society moving toward a watered down version of Christianity.

A FOUNDATION IN ALGEBRA

Faith is a subject many people are failing because "just believe" lacks context and conviction. The relational nature of God and the significance His book has on our daily lives is being missed. It's like the telephone game you played as a kid where the message whispered on one end didn't make it to the other end because too many people in the middle mixed up the content. We must get back to teaching the Word so that it lives on, true to the original message, the foundations.

My friend Kerry Moss, who was a huge inspiration for this book, told me *any teacher of Calculus will tell you that if you're not having success in Calculus, it's because your algebra and trigonometry aren't up to par. It's because your multiplication and division might be slow.*

In other words you can't do something complicated if you haven't mastered the basics.

Be it calculus or the Bible, truth only makes sense when you have the prerequisite, or foundation, to understand it.

Make sense? How can we be expected to be confident in a supernatural God who promises solutions to all the problems in our daily lives if we lack the foundation of how His Word got to us in the first place.

A SUPERNATURAL DOCUMENT

Here's that word again, supernatural. The problem, and it's a big one, is that many people have been led to believe that the Bible isn't supernatural, meaning not authored by God, but rather just old stories and parables told by regular men who had biases and prejudices. If that were the case then by all means, it's just a very well written piece of fiction. However we're told on several occasions by the Bible's most important authors that these are not their words but that of the one true God.

For I did not speak on my own, but the Father who sent me
commanded me to say all that I have spoken.
- The Apostle John

The word that came to Jeremiah from the Lord

"But to the married I give instructions, not I, but the Lord, that the
wife should not leave her husband.
Paul; 1 Corinthians 7:10.

Secular scholars have no trouble teaching history to be taken as truth, history that predates the birth of Christ. But when it comes to validating the Bible these same scholars often say they can't trust it.

Aside from the evidence supported in the *Did You Know* section at the end of each chapter, lets just take a common sense approach. I'd strongly argue that for people to say that simple men wrote the Bible by their own thoughts and on their own accord is actually way harder to believe than to say God did. Why? Well for the simple fact that they were simple men. Simple men who lived in a simple time, before text messaging, before high speed internet connections and before the fax machine or even the printing press. That makes it even more unrealistic that they would have been able to do such an amazing job of piecing everything together so articulately and accurately. It would have to be that they were all incredible geniuses, working in concert with one another and constantly checking one anothers finer points along the way.

Dare I say if you gathered Shakespeare, Twain, Tolstoy, Joyce, Hemingway, Kipling and Kafka and locked them in a room together for a year, or even two, and asked them to come up with a fictional story of creation, morality and salvation, that they would not be able to come close to matching the precision, beauty and intellectual wisdom of the Bible.

There is no error, no contradiction, no biases or imperfections, yet the Word is under constant attack.

Again, common sense tells me the Word wouldn't live this long, it wouldn't thrive as it has, change as many lives as it has if it were of the thoughts of mere men. Think about this, men have set out and devoted their entire lives to disproving it and in most instances, just the opposite happens, the doubters became the more ardent believers.

BLINDED ME WITH SCIENCE

One of the more embarrassing moments in my life was when Angelike and I were asked to come to our daughter's second grade classroom to read to the children at lunch. After reading Goldilocks and the Three Bears, I asked if there were any thoughts on the lesson. One boy toward the back of the class raised his hand and before he could get out the question, our daughter said, in a rather loud voice, "Dad, that's the boy who doesn't believe in Jesus. He believes in Science."

The innocent audacity of children. God bless her for her passion. Science and God do not exist absent one another, in fact quantum leaps in science over the last 100 years have done exactly the opposite of what one may think, rather than putting more distance between the two, it's actually brought them closer together.

Dr. Francis Collins, whose name gained household recognition during the pandemic as Director of the National Institute of Health, is associated with what many call the greatest scientific discovery in the history of mankind, the mapping of the human genome or DNA sequence. The Human Genome Project, which began in October of 1990 and completed in April 2003, gave us the ability, for the first time, to read nature's complete genetic blueprint for building a human being.

If any scientific discovery was to disprove the existence of intelligent design, this would definitely be the one. But in his book, *The Language of God*, Francis, a former atheist, then agnostic, tells about his journey to believer.

He writes: *"The God of the Bible is also the God of the genome. He can be worshiped in the cathedral or in the laboratory. His creation is majestic, awesome, intricate and beautiful - and it cannot be at war with itself. Only we imperfect humans can start such battles. And only we can end them."*

Interesting thought, that only human beings can end battles or wars. How about ending the fear of death? Ironically, the fear of death is the greatest weapon which man uses to assume power in the first place. Perhaps that's one reason why our public schools and our universities are taking God out of the classroom, teaching our young people that the Bible is just an old fashioned book written by a bunch of guys who made up stories using confusing language and parables. Somebody has to keep the next generation locked in fear and in line with the system by telling them lies. The truth is what will set them free.

STEP 2:
ONE BODY. ONE CHURCH

Isn't it the Church's responsibility to impress God's Word upon the next generation? That's what those who want to separate church and state argue. Sadly, many churches have done a pretty mediocre job teaching the Word of God and I know that stings to some and by saying it, I put a target on myself. Like Luther said, if you preach the gospel and don't specifically deal with the issues of our time, then you're not preaching it at all.

But pointing out the weakening of the Church is not my opinion, it's based on fact. A 2020 Gallup poll showed that church membership fell below 50 percent for the first time in 80 years, or since they began tracking it. Just 47 percent of Americans said they belong to a church whereas that number was 70 percent in 1999. We are seeing a steady decline defined by the generation of adults born before 1946 being the strongest (66% being affiliated with a church) compared to those in Generation X (50%) and then millennials (36%).

As a teenager going to church, I distinctly recall wondering why I wasn't more interested in going. I felt guilty if I didn't go but the desire wasn't there. I thought to myself, this can't be how Jesus taught. I can't imagine that drawing such devotion. What I'd later discover in life, is that there is power in the Word, and that it's awesome when it's presented in its original form, the way the Apostles taught it. It became obvious that we weren't teaching in a way that was engaging or clear, or with any context, particularly to young people. Because of this failure to communicate, we have a progressive fracturing of the church. The Great Apostasy, as it's called, is the falling away from the original faith founded by Jesus and promulgated through his twelve Apostles.

Luther wanted to correct the church, not splinter it and if there is a glaring vulnerability in Christianity, it's that its benevolent nature and desire to heal all who are sick, can sometimes be used against it. For instance, culture has influenced certain protestant religions into believing that God needs to evolve with mankind. They say the Word of God can morph into a more ambiguous document in order to be all inclusive.

Doesn't that, in itself, go against the very nature of Heaven? It's never mentioned in scripture as an all inclusive destination for "whatever you believe." In Matthew's Gospel, he tells us the gate is narrow and the road to destruction is wide. It's imperative not to get those two confused. Ultimately, these churches who stray from the truth have to decide if their job is to get more people into the church or into heaven.

THE ISMS

Dispensationalism, Hyperdispensationalism, Calvinsim, Humanism, Mysticism, Revivalism. All the "isms" of the Church must have non-believers asking is this faith or a Snoop Dog song.

And therein lies the problem or opportunity, depending on how you look at it. We can't lead people to God's Word by confusing them, remember overwhelm is our biggest problem. Most of these fractures of the church don't represent salvation issues as much as they do slight differences or opinions brought about by human interpretation. But others absolutely are salvation issues. I'd never want to lead somebody to Christianity only to have them be held up at the gate saying *"but David told me..."*

I'll reinstate that my goal is not to pick and choose, praise or condemn, but to ignite a deeper hunger for the truth of God's Word as it appears in scripture. I, David, may be wrong when it comes to interpreting scripture but the Word of God is infallible. This is a point I can't emphasize enough, we cannot change doctrine to fit into our culture, it must be presented properly, with relevance and context, and truth.

People don't want someone to open their mouth and shove it in. That approach doesn't convict most people, instead it repels them. I know because I've been there. It wasn't until Angelike and many others mentioned in this book prepared their knowledge with love, in such a way that made me say "wow, I never realized how that old book is so precisely woven together and how perfectly it relates to what's happening in my life now."

For me, a Church is more than just a building as most people see it, it encompasses God, Jesus and the Bible and everything filters through that.When there's a question, my first thought is always, let's see what the Bible says about that. That's what Jesus did, when he was confronted by the Devil, how did he answer? *"It is written."* When he was questioned by the Pharisees and Sadducees who were deliberately trying to trip him up, what did He do? He referred back to scripture.

People can argue theology, but the Word is written in a such a manner that we may use it for reproof, for correction and for instruction in righteousness so that the man of God may be perfect. (2 Timothy 3:16-17)

STEP 3: LEAD LIKE JESUS

As far back as I can remember I have always been fascinated by history, politics and religion and what I've witnessed over the last couple of decades has been that people were slowly being sold blurry versions of all three. Truth was being manufactured while at the same time it felt like we were being sold on a version of life that was "just okay," where we were being told that you'll have just enough to be happy with. In other words, here's vanilla, eat it and like it because it's for the greater good. But the last time I checked, people prefer options and they yearn for opportunity. That's why immigrants have flocked to the United States for almost 250 years, options in life and better opportunity for their family. But these things are not guaranteed without bold generational leadership and a foundation in God given rights.

We hold these truths to be self evident, that ALL men are CREATED equal, that they are endowed by their CREATOR with certain UNALIENABLE RIGHTS, that among these are LIFE, LIBERTY and THE PURSUIT of HAPPINESS.
July 4, 1776

There's that word again, pursuit. We were meant to be joyful, to pursue success, not to be at war with our neighbors or be sold a version of success that's small for you but grand for those in control. We were created as equals and so the mission of a generational leader is not just to gain knowledge and learn scripture but to instill wisdom and lead others so boldly that one's friends, neighbors and heirs comprehend God's message and fully prosper from it as well. Again, we see this type of bold leadership in the stories of Noah, Jeremiah, Esther, Deborah and David and certainly in Jesus.

> *"A leader is the one who knows the way,*
> *goes the way and shows the way"*
> *John C Maxwell*

Leaders lead by example, they don't tell people to do things they themselves would not do. They don't blindly incorporate laws or principles based on notoriety, riches or what's trending, but rather time tested wisdom and foundational truths set forth by God. Have you seen leaders of our time do this? Rarely.

Leaders of our day have been exposed for their *do as I say, not as I do* philosophies. We live in a world where we look at cheating as part of the game. In the realm of business, sports, and government, things have drifted toward a win at all costs philosophy, absent of morals and ethics. Our identity has become political rather than Biblical. It's a values inversion at nearly every level of society and you have it within your power to change it. What will you accept and what will you deny?

TERRA INCOGNITA

What we are waking up to every day in this world is unknown territory. Much of the American population has grown up privileged, with relative peace, but for the first time in our adult lives, we are faced with an enormous challenge. The call now goes out for Godly leadership in the home, in the marketplace and throughout all levels of government. Yes, you heard that right, it's a 180 degree reversal of everything you've been told about what's politically correct but it's the only way to battle the moral decay that has infested our world.

I can't imagine a parent alive who doesn't want the best for their child, who isn't concerned that the next generation will unwittingly concede basic human rights due to a lack of wisdom and deception. That's why we are witnessing an army full of moms and dads linking arms right now and standing up for future generations.

The question Angelike and I get quite often is how, how can we lead our family, our business and our community in a way that glorifies the Kingdom of God. I've always been a huge fan of simplicity and being in marketing, I think of the two great marketing campaigns of all time and how straightforward they were.

The first is Nike's *Just Do It*, it's simple, it's timeless and it applies to just about every single aspect of life. The second is *What Would Jesus Do?* and I love it for the same exact reasons. As you move toward the things which you desire to achieve most, a successful marriage, a happy family, contentment in work, building your community, leaving a legacy, the example Jesus sets is simple, timeless and applies to every aspect of your life. He knew the way and lived it and "knowing the way" always comes first. It's really the only order that works. With that being said, my advice is simple; know the way Jesus led. Study him as a mentor and how he went about his business and then just do it. Don't worry about who's watching, about what your circle of influence thinks or about being canceled.

Ask yourself, what would Jesus do and then just do that.

LAND OF CONFUSION

As we close this chapter regarding keeping it simple, let me remind you once again, we've chosen confusion and we can un-choose it as well. The only thing forcing you to feel overwhelmed is you. Free will. In a world where things seem to be going all wrong, it's time to focus on doing what's right. The key word being focus, something it's becoming harder and harder to do. It's so simple to be present and to do what's right. You know this.

Think about those days when you're on top of your game and your heart is in the right place. You puff your chest out and look up at God and say, "ok, I'm ready to co-create now" but then you get a text from your friend asking *did you see this*? Poof, you're out of creation and into distraction. Harvard researchers Matthew A. Killingsworth and Daniel T. Gilbert found that people spend 46.9% of their waking hours thinking about something other than what they're doing and so the first step in your quest for prosperity is understanding which areas of distraction you are most susceptible to. Is it on people and places far away or the minutia in your own home? Angelike reminds me, our battle begins in the home, with our sanctuary, this is where we can be so enticed by the distractions showing up on our devices that our attention often shifts to situations that don't concern us, robbing ourselves of precious moments with the people who need us most, right under our roof.

Because I can tend to be a "keyboard warrior" at times, she has also reminded me that *You fight from victory, not for victory,* that I must choose whether to let the enemy and his distraction mob steal my presence and rob her and our children of the moments that we have together or will I focus on building a foundation inside my home that others see at that light that cannot be hidden. To borrow from Matthew, can I build that *city on the hill* on my own plot of land, in my neighborhood, so that other houses and other people want to emulate it because it produces fruit.

MOMENTS BETWEEN MOMENTS

To be clear, I've not written this book to poke fun or vilify influencers, athletes, actors, musicians, politicians or you. Quite the opposite in fact. I've written it so that no matter who you are, the blinders may fall off your eyes and lead you back to the truth. Because it doesn't matter if you're Joe Rogan or Joe Schmo, we all have moments in between the moments, tiny everyday experiences between the big exciting moments that we need to find meaning in. That doesn't mean we become oblivious to what's happening in the world, but we have to decide where our energy is best served.

The reality of life is that be it a night at the Super Bowl or the Super 8, the red carpet or Red Lobster, the delivery of the royal baby or the delivery at your front porch, there is something called everyday life and we're missing out on it. We're missing out on it because we've become victims to distraction. Nobody, be you a prince or a pauper, escapes it. We all have a walk we do at home, when nobody is watching or taking photos, when the outside world is closed off, and that is the space where we have to find deeper meaning to life and real connection by way of a loving bond that lasts. God does his best work and most important work in the home.

By wisdom a house is built, and by understanding it is established;
by knowledge the rooms are filled with all precious and pleasant riches.
Proverbs 24: 3-4

Precious and pleasant riches means something different to each of us and we have to define what that is. I said it in my first book and it's worth repeating here, there is nothing like the feeling of longing for one more conversation with a parent who is no longer with you or that of a parent who wishes they had their children back home for one more night, to hear the sound of tiny footsteps scurrying around the floor.

We have to ask ourselves if we've fallen victim to a values inversion, are we wasting our presence on people who serve us or things which steal our joy. If all you have to look forward to are things you do or buy and the anticipation of how your audience on social media will react to them, sooner or later you're going to be awakened to a rude reality, because you'll always need more things to feel fulfilled, and they can be taken away, leaving us vulnerable.

Don't get me wrong, I like nice things and I love to go to nice places, but my focus and attention must first be placed on the people in closest proximity to me, setting aside time for investing, shaping, planning, and giving life to them. It's what our Turned On philosophy is almost entirely based on, and yet it still takes massive intention on a daily basis. It's a practice.

So as we build this case for prosperity, let's remember there are always going to be lulls to the lifestyle and halts in the hustle and a large majority of people are missing the meaning of life by focusing so much of their time on little gods on little screens rather than the big issues and big God in their homes.

Don't continue to play in the lower levels of creation, chasing after worldly validation. As Joel Brown stated in the foreword, that is not where God wants you. He doesn't want you frustrated, running about in doubt or in debt. He doesn't want his children feeling a lack of purpose because they've fallen into constant comparison with people who are basically strangers. God wants you to step into your power, the power he has promised, because when you begin to do that, being present with those around you, then you'll see how obvious it is, God's story really is all around me, it's my story too.

DID YOU KNOW?

There are 1,239 prophecies found in the Old Testament and 578 prophecies in the New Testament, for a total of 1,817. In the book *Science Speaks,* Peter Stoner uses mathematics and modern science to establish the probability of fulfilling just eight of the 300 prophecies pertaining to Jesus Christ in the Bible.

He says, "The chance that any man might have fulfilled all eight prophecies is one in 10 to the 17th power. That would be 1 in 100,000,000,000,000,000." (one hundred quadrillion). Stoner said "that would be equivalent to covering the whole state of Texas with silver dollars two feet deep and then expecting a blindfolded man to walk across the state and on the very first try find the ONE coin you marked."

One of the most remarkable Bible prophecies in my opinion is that found in Mark 13:1-2 where Jesus prophesied the destruction of the Jewish Temple saying to his disciples; *"There will not be left here one stone upon another that will not be thrown down." (Mark 13:1-2)*

Just thirty seven years after Jesus made the prediction, the Roman Emperor Titus took Jerusalem by siege and burned the temple to the ground (70 AD). Today, if you go to Jerusalem you will see massive pieces of stone scattered across the ground like Legos. It's mind boggling to think how one of the greatest structures in all of the ancient world was reduced to rubble.

The Jewish Temple was a marvel of architecture, and to give you some scale, the smallest stones were 2 to 5 tons and the largest being 570 tons. It was built by 1,000 masons and 10,000 laborers.

The walls above ground rose ten stories tall, and their foundations were as deep as 20 meters in some places. Josephus, the most well known historian outside of biblical scholars, describes one of the stones in the foundation as being sixty-seven by seven by nine feet and that the stones of the temple were thirty-seven by twelve by eighteen feet in size.

The entire temple complex measures about 1.5 million square feet.

Josephus was the equivalent to a modern day war correspondent and he describes the Romans siege of the Temple in horrific detail; *For one would have thought that the hill itself, on which the temple stood, was seething hot; as full of fire on every part of it, that the blood was larger in quantity than the fire, and those that were slain, more in number than those that slew them. For the ground did no where appear visible, for the dead bodies that lay on it.*

CHAPTER 10

BRICK HOUSE

"God Is Not the Author of Confusion, but of Peace"
1 Corinthians 14:33

When people take my course, it's to grow their business and make them more profitable. I love helping people increase their wealth, but my first goal is to get them out of a poverty mindset, and that's probably not what you think.

Typically, when we speak of poverty, the first thing that comes to mind is a lack of money, but the Word of God speaks to the poor in spirit and in my experience I've found it extremely hard, if not impossible, to help people increase their wealth when their spirit is weak and under attack.

If you've ever tried to take your pants off over your shoes or put your sneakers on while the laces were still tied it can be extremely frustrating. Why, because that's not the order you're supposed to do things in. It doesn't make sense, so when *The Bachelor* doesn't work out with the bride, the trillion dollar government spending doesn't fix the poverty problem or the four-pump coffee doesn't fix your energy crisis we shouldn't be surprised. We know it's a flawed approach that completely goes against the natural order.

The same philosophy holds true when it comes to creating a happy home and business, it helps if you take your time and pay attention to the order.

A DIVINE ORDER

There are three things needed when building something, a foundation, materials and labor.

There's a reason why the majority of the stories found in scripture are not about perfect people, because at its heart, it's a relational document. It's why it's helped so many people dig themselves out of dark places. Scripture is full of narratives containing flawed sinners who made major mistakes, they committed adultery, they stole, they cheated and they even murdered. All the big life stressors are covered: love, health, family, business, pain, disappointment, jealousy, you name it.

They all point to a single narrative, a Kingdom down approach, aka a divine order. It's important to remember the goal of reading the Bible is to uncomplicate what the world insists on complicating, to restore to wholeness what has been fractured.

Skim the bookstore aisle or flip through instagram and search for a "coach" or an "expert" and you won't have a problem finding one. I've read a lot of books, hired dozens of experts and attended scores of conferences. I've even walked on fire. But after all that, Angelike and I still found ourselves beat up and embattled. We couldn't coach or lead the way we'd been taught anymore because the foundation was shaking.

I distinctly remember Angelike, several years ago, telling me how burnt out and bogged down she felt with the endless rabbit hole of advice. She said "David, I feel like God is being left out and that's what is missing. I hear the Holy Spirit whispering to me, 'put Me in coach.' He's telling us to bring Him into the marketplace, the one place people advise specifically to leave Him out."

So we started to do our research. Who were the most followed, loved and valuable "coaches" out there who were also using biblical principles, some of whom I've mentioned in this book. We also started to wake up to the fact that in the secular world of business, there was really nothing new under the sun and people were being encouraged to *stop playing small* with having no foundational truth for what playing big meant.

BIG TIME
I'm on my way, I'm making it

You've heard it a thousand times before, "stop playing small." It sounds good, but can anybody really tell you what it means?

It's vague and obtuse and there's a great deal of that floating around these days, especially in entrepreneurial circles where that type of cliche seems to thrive. Imagine a new coach walking into the New York Knicks or Cleveland Browns locker room on day one saying "Ok fellas, we need to stop playing small."

Yea coach, thanks, we never thought of that.

What if the President took to the podium to give the State of the Union Address and said "We've got to stop playing small."

Can you give me some context?

Pardon my sarcasm, but it's rarely defined.

My definition of how to stop playing small is to start acknowledging the Creator of everything big and develop a reverence for his style of architecture and how He built. Before you can *step into your power*, consider giving a nod to His.

In Genesis we can clearly see a formula for creation. We learn first that God was aware and saw a void. Seems rather straightforward but I've witnessed too many divorces that occured because couples went right into creation or multiplying, i.e. buying new cars, new floors or having more babies, before the awareness of the void and chaos. In business, have you ever witnessed somebody put their website up before really establishing the content for their area of expertise?

The next thing God does is bring light to a situation. When you have a circumstance in front of you where you need to create something or course correct, there needs to be light. In Genesis 1:3 this is not the sunlight, it's energy, a physical manifestation of power, the spark of life, the ruach. Genesis 1:14 was the light in the vault of the sky or sun and moon.

In my interpretation of the divine order, as it appears in our lives, it relates directly to the collaborative forces generated between intention and will power. To be more specific, as a Christian entrepreneur and husband, it means taking whatever gleam or sparkle God has put in my heart and acting obediently on it. Listening to what God says over to what the world is telling you.

Angelike and I have built our entire brand around that thought.

You are the light of the world. A town built on a hill cannot be hidden. Neither do people light a lamp and put it under a bowl. Instead they put it on its stand, and it gives light to everyone in the house. In the same way, let your light shine before others, that they may see your good deeds and glorify your Father in heaven.
Matthew 5:14-16

The next step in the divine order is an establishment of the environment. If we look at the verbs in Genesis, God separated and gathered and when we take our blueprints from the master creator we see how important this is.

We, as human beings, have many weaknesses and as I've pointed out several times, our inability to reduce the overwhelm in order to get really focused is the biggest weakness. We may very well have the will to do something but do we have the right environment? Our environment is often stronger than our will power, so no matter how strong your desire is to get in shape, you can't establish a healthy diet with a refrigerator that's a mess and a grill that's out of gas. Likewise, in a marriage, if things aren't going as you would like, you can't just snap your fingers and expect change to happen. Once you become aware and decide to put the energy in, you also have to establish the right environment so you can course correct.

If it's a communication problem, you can't start blaming work or the children or your in-laws. The issue might be lack of quality time together and the only way to fix that is to separate those things from one another and then gather together.

In work, there's no functionality in a chaotic environment. You've heard the devil loves a mess. Some of my most frustrating moments in writing this book have come when I've failed to maintain the environment around my desk or within my computer, so when I needed something like a notebook or a certain paragraph, I couldn't find them. This leads to frustration.

We often invite chaos into our lives because we're busy, that's when things get piled up. But it's exasperated by the fact we've been conditioned to seek pleasure first. Our modern world is so pleasure focused, we get things out of order, people try to find joy before they fix themselves or their environment. It's like moving into a new home and putting up the flat screen and watching Netflix while all the boxes are still lying around unpacked. There must be order.

The next phase of the divine order is establishing relationship. In Genesis 1:26 God creates mankind, animals and plants so they would have relationship and functionality to one another. We now see how important setting up our environment is to setting up success. Now that your refrigerator is organized, your date night is scheduled and your desktop is clean, you can work on the relationship with food (the cooking), the relationship with your spouse (the intimacy) and the relationship to your work (clean, clear thinking) and progress.

As I said before, other belief systems fall short because they simply can't define relationship. However the Word says "God sees", "God hears" and "God Brings forth" because there is a complimentary or mutual relationship between the creator and what He has created. It is written. Therefore, in a house or business built on the divine order, it's critical that relationship exists. The opposite of this would be to ignore, tune out or withhold from your home or business God's input. Actions opposed to morality, ethics and discipline are cause for some of the greatest conflict in your life.

God blessed them and said to them,
"Be fruitful and increase in number; fill the earth and subdue it."
Genesis 1:28

The next part of the divine order is to produce. It's easy to see how people get out of order and put this first. You get excited by a podcast or event you attended and you rush home to get productive but your mind can't think straight because your environment is not set up to support you, as in: your diet is giving you brain fog, your spouse isn't supporting your dreams, and that notebook with all those contacts and notes is nowhere to be found. The order has got you in a bind now. What do you do next? Look at God's example, we (man) were his most important creation, if I may take liberty to guess that He was most excited to produce us, His greatest ambition. But did he make us first? No. He had to take care of the heavens, the light, the waters, the stars, vegetation, and the animals. He had to set Adam up in the right environment for success. He couldn't throw Him into chaos.

Lead by your maker's example. We are all created to expand His creation, to take the talents and gifts bestowed upon us and to combine them with His word, taking them into our homes and the marketplace. If we don't steward them, we run the risk of dying spiritually each day, never being able to put a finger on why we feel resentful or bored or why we feel like we are chasing a moving target.

In the second to last paragraph of Genesis 1, God says He gives it all to us - *everything that has the breath (ruach) of life in it.* That is where co-creation is defined in scripture, it exists in everything that inspires, motivates, encourages, stirs, provokes, stimulates and *everything that influences.*

The final part of the divine order is most likely everybody's favorite, to celebrate and to rest. This is why God created the sabbath because when you are finished and everything is good, it's time to acknowledge what you've accomplished and rest because through and with God you have done it, in adherence to the divine order. You've earned the rest. Just like God rested after each day in the story of creation.

AGAINST THE WIND

For a long time, Angelike and I fed off the woo woo platitudes and motivational speeches of the secular world, which always left us walking away feeling a bit phony to put it bluntly. Eventually things like *analysis paralysis* and *fake it til ya make it* rolled off our shoulders and we began to yawn hearing about the 9,000 shots Michael Jordan missed in his career for the ten thousandth time.

And at the other end, we grew tired of churches who just told people to pray for abundance and prosperity and somehow checks would appear in their mailbox. We grew weary of adhering more to ritual than to relationship. More recital than retention.

Be it church or business, the engineered sound bites we so willingly wrote down and repeated got us nowhere, other than to make for a lot of notepads lying around the house. We begrudgingly sang in church and clapped at conferences only to wind up at the end of the day with nothing to show in regard to a true foundation of happiness.

It's easy to get caught between two paradigms, on one end there was always a spiritual emptiness despite being wealthy in our bank account and on the other end an earthly emptiness despite partaking in religious festivities on Sunday. We had to admit that we had failed, in spite of our best intentions, to become enlightened. We failed because we had the wrong dream.

So we made a decision to start over. Not completely, but from a philosophical point of view. In my heart, I believe people are inherently good and altruistic in nature but along the way we get lost and distracted by shiny objects that intermittently corrupt our judgment. I wanted to be part of the solution to getting more people acting out of integrity than imitation. That begins with recognizing the good in God's plan and praising it.

Ok, so what's that have to do with the divine order you ask? As you know, this is not an easy time to build anything in our world. We're all being stretched to our capacity in so many ways. In our professional circles of building we hear the parts aren't here or the labor isn't available. At home we're trying to stay focused on normalcy in a world that is anything but normal.

Whatever the reason, our ability to create both literally and figuratively has been compromised. In this new season of uncertainty, under the guise of being woke, the world has really been put to sleep. In a desire to make everybody feel accepted, give everybody a trophy and apply everybody's truth, we lost the ability to tell right from wrong, to endure the agony of defeat and to seek eternal truth.

So we have to go back to the very beginning, like Genesis, when everything was in chaos. Remember, not a reset, or a reimagine but a revival. And in order to spark that feeling in you, allow me to ask this; when were you last innocent? Meaning when can you recall creating with the mind of a child, unaware of what anybody thought or what would become of it. When did you create just for the sake of creating? Your childhood, yes? Painter Pablo Picasso said *It took me four years to paint like Raphael, but a lifetime to paint like a child.*

The optimism of childhood. If you're a parent then surely you've watched your child look at life's simplest things in amazement. You think to yourself, they have no idea what's going on, no idea what country is invading another or who is threatening to impeach who. You wonder, they must just be thinking how can I stack the Tupperware or tear down the bookshelf today. Either way, it's pure exploration and I think it must be how God initially designed our story. Here's a garden, go explore and create.

Take that thought and fast forward to today, be it a job, a relationship or a diet, you started something that was founded or forged in innocence but it drifted away. You began something with pure imagination but somewhere along the journey you were either subjected to temptation, corruption or maybe just poor judgment.

What happened is that you lost sight of the wonder of creation and what it means to be innocent. Consider this, you don't find many people exchanging rings at the altar saying I can't wait to hate and argue with you someday. You didn't join the company thinking one day I'll curse the fact that I have to get out of bed and come here. And believe it or not, I truly think even the most unethical lawmakers of our time got into politics because of an authentic desire to help and make the world a better place.

I believe this because by nature, we are born or start off innocent and become subject to corruption from the people we surround ourselves with. By human nature, we get comfortable and let our guard down, even Eve knew the serpent well enough not to run from him when he approached her. And remember this, despite how artists have painted it over the years, the enemy was not relegated to his belly yet, so clear and present danger wasn't the case.

Like most of our mistakes, we lost sight of God's plan or divine order. Eve chose to ignore the truth and let her comfort and curiosity take precedence over order. Order says, go back to the beginning, what was the environment and relationship supposed to be like? Paradise, yes? You have to ask, how does paradise get so boring that you'd risk losing it? The answer is that somebody convinced you there was something better, something you were missing, that the grass was greener on the other side. Isn't that why we lose our innocence in this, our present day? It's the reason for divorce, depression and even war. We are convinced to ignore the simple beauty and simple instructions and so we break a law or commandment.

Keep this Book of the Law always on your lips; meditate on it day and night, so that you may be careful to do everything written in it.
Then you will be prosperous and successful.
(Joshua 1:7)

How's that for a straightforward and uncomplicated message? Meditate on it and just do it. That's where prosperity is.

Accountability is very clear in Genesis. The very first thing Adam and Eve lost was innocence and for the first time they noticed they were naked. Adam said he was afraid because he noticed his state and then he tried to shift the blame to Eve. Some partner huh? But not just Eve, Adam blamed God, *the woman YOU put here with me.* Then the woman does what, shifts the blame to the serpent. It was his fault she ate the fruit.

If we are to rebuild our house by reviving the Word, we must emphasize this most important lesson of accepting responsibility. We have to stop placing the blame on other people. Culture is intent on giving us a thousand excuses and fingers to point at for our lack of happiness and right there in Joshua is the answer, *do everything written in this book.* It's that simple.

THESE ARE MY PEOPLE

Most of the people I work with are transitioning in one way or another. They're going from one season of life to another, one state to another or one career to another. My conclusion is always the same, regardless if it's a career or belief system you're in search of, which is; the confidence in the wisdom or advice you seek is in direct proportion to its source. Who is at the head of your decision making process and what is their foundation based on? If they choose me as a coach, I am simply a conduit for God's order and I always point them to the wisdom in the Word first.

For example, people will tell me "But I've been doing this job half my life, so I'm not sure how to transition." That's not true, I say. You know how to transition, you just lack faith in your ability." If people tell me they have trouble in their marriage and they don't know how to change, I say no, you're just being prideful and running from a tough conversation. If people would tell me they can't take the lead in their company or their home because they don't know if they are capable, my response is, "no, you're just comfortable." All those lessons were taught to me from scripture.

I wish it were that easy though. The enemy of your soul will always seize an opportunity to keep you from the scope and breadth of God's plans to prosper you, and this happens by deception in the form of false idols, who want to keep you comfortable and keep you in the spirit of pride by telling you to run when you should be turning to face the challenge.

You cannot allow, at any cost, those seeds of doubt to negate what God says about you and how to fix your problems. I cannot say it any clearer that you must be as stubborn as a ram when the devil tries to offer you something else and remember that you belong to God, you have been chosen.

> 'You shall be My people, And I will be your God.'
> Jeremiah 30:22

One of the biggest misconceptions we can make is believing that there is some giant chasm that exists between those who call themselves Christians and those who don't. What I mean is that the human thread is that we all want to know that we matter and that our lives have meaning. I know we all get that because we nearly had a civil war almost over whose lives mattered most. The news played passionate speeches about the value of human life from community leaders and elected officials but it became political theater, another means to distract and overwhelm us. What many people left out was the divine authority of God.

Those who seek God and call themselves Christains have a foundation for knowing we all matter to Him. It's that simple.

We all matter and we're all born with dreams. At a young age you may have scribbled yourself in crayon as a firefighter, an astronaut, a veterinarian or a baseball player. As you got older, you encountered different things which tempted your spirit and tested your convictions. It's called adversity and it's part of life. Sometimes adversity comes in the form of other people, somebody hurt you, somebody chastised you, somebody questioned your intentions or abilities. Sometimes we chase adversity as a blind quest for self destruction. We step out of bed and turn on our television or smartphone and engage people trying to tell us what to do, how to act, who to follow and what to believe. Regardless of which type, they both have a significant effect on our ability to keep our attention focused on what matters and stay on the right path.

Each day people wake up and chase the giant red X, the kind like you see on a treasure map which reads *you've arrived*. But it doesn't exist. That's not reality. Problems don't go away, success is not final. In any 90-day game plan, there will always be day 91.

The reality for all of us is that we're being distracted and deceived to focus on an earthy destination rather than a heavenly one. A good friend of mine said something that hit home in regard to this. He has six young children and he said "I want them to be happy. I want them to enjoy life and grow up to be successful and have a home and family of their own one day. However, my number one priority is to get them to Heaven." Think about that. When do you hear anything so profound from the people leading our schools and country right now? We've missed the most important goal of all time.

The reality is that our children are growing up before our eyes. The reality is there is always room for a deeper connection in our marriages. The reality is culture is tearing down the family and culture is tearing down our communities. And the final reality is if we don't build up and we continue to tear down, we won't recognize what's left of our world.

If any of that sounds familiar, if you've ever found yourself waking up every day and walking around in some sort of ambiguity, asking yourself *Is this it? Is this all life has to offer? Am I embarking on a relentless pursuit of achievement and endless quest for consumption?* You're not alone, Angelike and I can relate.

Don't get me wrong, it wasn't that life was bad, it just didn't fill our cups. We found ourselves simply connecting the dots between moments of happiness, but in the moments between moments, in between the business launches and time under the lights speaking on stage, there was an equal amount of angst and apathy, we were either stressing to hit a goal or lethargic in our approach to everything that wasn't one.

HUNGRY LIKE THE WOLF

When the movie the Wolf of Wall Street hit theaters, it was the buzz of the entrepreneurial world. And because Jordan Belfort (played by Leonardo DiCaprio) was aggressive by nature and cussed like a sailor, a lot of people modeled that behavior. But just because the world has lost its innocence, doesn't mean we have to in order to be competitive in it.

The Word says to be alert and of sober mind, and when you find yourself in a situation or place that you don't belong, when your intuition taps you on the shoulder and says something feels wrong, listen to it, it's discernment speaking to you. Discernment is a gift of the Holy Spirit and a tool more valuable than any other in today's world.

Angelike and I have witnessed first hand good people become subject to corruption, either as willing participants or through willful ignorance, meaning they just pretended not to see it. Paul warned the early church of this saying ***do not be misled, bad company corrupts good character.*** We cannot claim to be ignorant of what is good, that's how we got here, massive apathy. People stopped calling out those who were doing wrong until corruption just became a way we understood business and government to work.

LET'S STAY TOGETHER

I hope you're getting this message, what God creates for good, the devil will try to counterfeit and destroy in order to tear down. So when culture tries to pit man against woman, black against white and left against right, that's not God, that's the enemy. Division leads to destruction.

We have to know not just the book of the Lord but the Lord of the book. Jesus was neither white with blue eyes, nor black with brown, but most likely somewhere in between. Jesus' first appearance after his death was to a woman and God spoke first to a young Mary about his plan, not Joseph. It was Pontius Pilate's wife who was bold and warned him not to get involved in the trial of Jesus. And in Proverbs 4:27 it literally says *do not turn to the right or to the left: remove thy foot from evil.*

Going back to Abraham Lincoln, he said *A house divided against itself, cannot stand.* This is where the true calling of the Church must be, united as one body in this battle against culture and man's desire to possess authority over man. Wisdom is the only thing that can set us free.

When I pray with my daughters each night we say *Heavenly Father, I thank you for letting me define who I am and who I am not through your wisdom and your words and not through the eyes of culture.*

God's word is in trouble right now and that is why you must guard yourself with the fact that when you speak truth and others reject it or criticize you for it, it's not so much as a personal attack on you but an attack on *the God in you.*

DID YOU KNOW?

Scholars claim the Gospel of Luke and the Book of Acts were written between 60 and 62 AD, meaning just 27 years after the crucifixion of Jesus.

The Bible has been translated to over 690 languages.

'The Lord of the Rings' by J. R. R. Tolkien has sold 150 million copies in 68 years.

The Holy Bible sells over 100 million copies every year.

More than 66,000 people are using a Bible app at any given second.

Three people share a Bible verse on their social network every second.

In 1900, 80% of the world's Christians lived in Europe or the United States.

Today, 60% of Christians live in the developing world.

The Bible mentions 49 women by name.

There are more than 3,000 prophecy verses in the Bible that have already came true in some way. Around 3,000 more prophecies are yet to come to completion.

The shortest sentence in the Bible is, "Jesus wept," (John 11:35)

"Lord" is the most common word in the Bible, it is used in the Old Testament over 7000 times, and another 600-700 times in the New Testament.

The last word in the Bible is "Amen"

CHAPTER 11

FOR THE LOVE OF MONEY

"The world runs on individuals pursuing their separate interests. The record of history is absolutely clear, there is no alternative way, so far discovered, of improving the lives of ordinary people that can hold a candle to the productive activities that are unleashed by a free enterprise system."

- Milton Friedman

Nobel Prize Winning Economist

If you want to step into an interesting conversation, sit down with a group of Christians and ask them about being rich. Chances are you'll hear more than one person recite that famous line "Money is the root of all evil."

I've seen priests who preached that money was evil and pastors who preached the prosperity gospel, which is Jeremiah 29:11 absent of context. They were both wrong. What I can tell you for sure is that for the Body of Christ to make a revival, we have to start talking about Biblical stewardship of wealth and go back to what the Word says about money.

It's not evil. How can money be the root of all evil when 1 out of 10 verses in the Gospels deals with money? In 16 out of 38 of Jesus' parables he speaks of riches and possessions. In fact, nearly 25 percent of Jesus' words in the New Testament deal with biblical stewardship.

The Bible specifically says *"For the **LOVE OF** money is a root of all kinds of evil."* (1 Timothy 6:10) It doesn't say having money is evil. Can you see what a huge difference a few words can make? That is why in several spots in the Bible it mentions do not add or take anything away from this book. By adding LOVE OF, everything in the context changes and biblical scripture without context is dangerous.

If you have a strong desire to earn money and create a fruitful life for your family, is that evil? No. If you say you want to work extra hard and earn a lot of money, is that evil? No. Then why is there such a disconnect between the church and the marketplace? Because more people have to shine a light on what's right and break the darkness of deception. We, as the church, shouldn't accept broke people in the pews any more than we should accept spiritually bankrupt people on Wall Street.

Let's put an emphasis on meeting both with equal enthusiasm so we can set a strong foundation for future generations of Americans.

I'll begin by giving you a better context, let's go to back to Paul who, during his ministry, warns his young pupil Timothy of wealth's trap saying ***beware of the pursuit of riches as many who pursue gold fall also into the temptations of other foolish lusts that accompany that pursuit, ultimately leading men to drown in destruction and perdition.***

It's as if somebody said football is evil. Really? No, it's not you'd say, but you should beware of going to a football game because people there can drink too much and get in fights and you might be tempted to gamble on it and get into debt. So is the game itself bad? No. What if you watch a lot of football? Still not bad. It's what can happen if you're not careful and let football become your idol.

We can also compare it to some Christian's views on sex. There are those who say that sex is the tool of the devil. No, that would be untrue as well. Proverbs tells us *"rejoice in the wife of your youth.. let her breasts fill you at all times with delight; be intoxicated always in her love."* To say sex is bad is a broad brush with no context, which contradicts the Word of God and contradicts procreation as well.

Again, let's look to Paul who, in his wisdom, provides a deeper context telling married people in 1st Corinthians *"Do not deprive one another, except perhaps by agreement for a limited time, that you may devote yourselves to prayer; but then come together again, so that Satan may not tempt you because of your lack of self-control."*

Paul's words couldn't be any clearer. Sex is for marriage and it's healthy. Husband and wife should not deprive one another of sex because that leaves a door open for the devil to sneak in and corrupt something beautiful which God gave us.

As our conversation turns toward how you can achieve prosperity, there has to be context with the understanding that the poor in spirit and poor in their bank account are related. I don't believe it does the Kingdom any good to have miserable, financially broken people talking about pushing through to victory the same way it doesn't do it any good to have rich people with corrupt morals speak of it. The emphasis of scripture is to lead a balanced, fruitful life, with your eyes on God first.

As I mentioned Paul's thoughts on money and sex, it's important to know that it is not his philosophy nor his wisdom but God's. In Galatians, Paul very clearly tells us *I did not receive (these words) from any man, nor was I taught it; rather, I received it by revelation from Jesus Christ* meaning this is a relational God speaking to us, telling us ways to overcome some of life's biggest dilemmas. It's neither money nor sex which is sinful but rather the lust for them apart from God which is. That's a message God needs us to hear and one that I'd say religion is missing the bar on.

What do 99 percent of the scandals we hear about in life deal with? Sex and money. If the devil had a six-shooter, those would be the first two bullets, so imagine our world if more people were given God's wisdom when it came to those issues. Where do you think we'd be as a culture? Don't you think we could save some marriages, and in turn, save families and communities as a ripple effect.

ONE LOAF OF BREAD

Let's go a bit further and provide more evidence of what money means from a biblical perspective. We will begin with the Hebrew word Dam (Dawm) which means blood. The ancient plural of this word is Damim (Da-meem) which is the word for money or payment. The connection is that the two represent livelihood, a natural flow of things necessary to secure life.

Life, as we know it here on earth, doesn't exist without the circulation of blood and for just about all of man's existence life hasn't existed without commerce (money) either. As blood gives life circulating through the body, so does money give life circulating through the economy. What happens when either is taken away? Death. If money is taken out of the economy, you have financial death. If blood is taken from the body, you have physical death.

As a culture, we're doing a very poor job dissecting the Word of God and teaching young people how to steward money and as a culture, we continue to elect people who do a very poor job keeping money circulating. Borrowing and/or printing is not good as we are about to find out. Now I understand that there are a lot of people who might say that it's not the Church's job to teach money principles but then you'd have to ask why money is such an integral component of scripture? It's in the Bible because it's critical to life and our livelihood. Listen to these words by Peter Grandich, author of *Confessions of a Wall Street Wiz Kid* who says: *"The writers of the Bible anticipated the problems we would have with money and possessions. (That is why) I get my financial guidance from the Bible. Money and possessions are the second most referenced topic in the Bible – and the message is clear: Nowhere in Scripture is debt viewed in a positive way."*

The question goes back to one of the most familiar Bible passages there is, are we teaching people to fish or just giving fish away?

NOWHERE IN SCRIPTURE IS DEBT VIEWED IN A POSITIVE WAY

Debt is a form of enslavement and it has always been a means to control people. Remember the very first pages of this book? I mentioned that despite their promises, our politicians, year in and year out, continue to increase the Federal Deficit. A deficit is a liability and who in their right mind would willingly saddle their children with liability?

If you've ever said the Lord's Prayer, which is found in both Matthew and Luke's gospels, then you know the line *"Forgive us our **trespasses**, as we forgive those who **trespass** against us."* In the King James Version of the Bible, it reads *"forgive us our **debts** as we forgive our **debtors**."* The two words are interchangeable in the prayer because when we have financial debt, it requires payment the same way sin requires a payment, the price of which Jesus assumed for us on the cross. So debt is a metaphor for sin.

In the secular world, you're familiar with phrases like being *"chained to a mortgage"* or *"handcuffed to a car payment."* Growing up, you may have heard your mother or father sigh *"we're buried under all these bills."* Clearly there is an association between money and enslavement, even death. In regard to this book, any attempt to prosper (tsalach/push forward) without being able to prosper (succeed financially) is not only unreasonable, but it's not Biblical.

Finance expert Dave Ramsey so eloquently puts it, *"**managing God's blessings, God's ways for God's glory.**"* Do for him so that he may do with you what is good. Christian author Lynn A Miller writes *"**Stewardship is the act of organizing your life so that God can spend you.**"* That right there should give you and your family a solid definition of what co-creating with God is defined as. Stamp that into your memory bank or print it out and tape it to the refrigerator. It's one of the most valuable things you can give your children to have both a fulfilling life here on earth as well as the one to come.

If you are faithful in obeying God's commandments,
you will be blessed and able to lend and not borrow.
Deuteronomy 15:6

When people tell me the Bible is complicated or confusing, I point them to a verse like this and say "tell me how." Follow God's rules and you're blessed, fall to the deception of culture's rules and you're likely to be enslaved in sin (debt). When a large part of a society goes into debt so deep, they slowly (the gradual road) become subservient to a government (ruling class) who controls the resources and thus has power over them. That's all debt is after all, giving an entity dominion over you. It means that you are not free or that your liberty is at stake.

During the pandemic, I was never worried about the virus or the lockdowns as much as I was about the economy. At first that sounds insensitive but I know human nature and in general, people possess the resolve to fight sickness and brave boredom, but take away their means to feed their families and now you have people willing to do things they normally wouldn't consider and thus susceptible to the power and control of an authority other than God.

Democratic strategist James Carville became famous during the 1992 election by saying, "it's the economy stupid," and rightly so, becasue that's always where people are most concerned and most vulnerable.

NO MONEY, MO PROBLEMS

To reiterate, despite our best intentions, we often do things contrary to what makes the most sense because we are taking our direction from a fairy tale world where the same mistakes are repeated over and over.

Fool me once, shame on me, fool me every four years, shame on all of us. Man's wisdom versus God's is a very one sided score card and God always wins, but we aren't listening to God, we're falling for the fairy tale.

If we don't open scripture and teach our children how money is tied to their liberty and the proper ways to earn and save it, then we're in the land of make-believe and we just keep drinking the potion. Big banks, big government and the student loan industry, prefer to keep borrowers ignorant and in debt. It's a Ponzi scheme and in the Old Testament it's referred to as *usury*, where lending money to a "brother" at any rate of interest was always forbidden.

He (who) lends at interest and takes a profit. Will such a man live?
He will not! Because he has done all these detestable things,
he is to be put to death; his blood will be on his own head.
Ezekiel 18:13

If you are reading this for the first time, that might be shocking, but there is no mincing of words - detestable is quite clear. Surely this tugs at everything you've understood about how money, the economy and capitalism works. You might say, of course there has to be lending and interest, that's why we have mortgages and car loans and a Fed who regulates interest rates. It's just how the world works.

Not necessarily. It's how the world has worked since 1913 when the Federal Reserve was created. If you're reading this, you weren't around back then so this system is all you know. But there are the two questions you always need to ask - who are you following or taking your direction from and what type of fruit has that advice bared?

In his book *The Creature from Jekyll Island*, G. Edward Griffin writes *"Since its inception, (The Fed) has presided over the crashes of 1921 and 1929; the Great Depression of '29 to '39; recessions in '53, '57, '69, '75, and '81; a stock market "Black Monday" in '87."*

That's not a great track record, but what are we always told by the power players who control the money? That it's a "necessary reset" of the market. There's that word again, reset. My ears perk up when I hear it because it's not good.

Griffin adds *"The new business model for America is clearly recognizable. Its dominant feature is the merger of government, real estate, and commerce into a single structure, tightly controlled at the top. It is the same model used in Soviet Russia, Nazi Germany, Fascist Italy, and Communist China."*

That's quite a heavy accusation is it not? To be honest, as a life-long Capitalist, it made me stop to think, are we truly in a free market or does there seem to be a deception of that? The Center For Responsible Lending reports that 91 percent of all payday loans are made to repeat borrowers. That doesn't resemble *damim*, a natural flow of money, more like a cycle stuck on repeat. In looking for ways to prosper our families and live free, we should look to scripture for answers for the right reasons. We're handcuffed in by a mortgage and buried in debt because we've been deceived into thinking debt and interest is just a normal way to live and that more of it doesn't make much difference.

MONEY FOR NOTHING

If we look at the Book of Acts, it tells us all the believers sold their possessions and shared everything. Socialists love to point to this part of the Bible and will claim that were Jesus alive today, he would lean toward Socialism.

That's deception. The problem with socialism is that it deprives people of the very co-creation with God I've been speaking of all along. The first thing it does is strip the individual of their ambition and discourages creativity all for the sake of the "greater good," an intentionally deceptive term we've seen rise in popularity. Socialism has gained steam in America because it's packaged in a vacuum, meaning the idea might sound appealing but it's not practical in a land of dreamers strewn across three and a half million miles. A nation of 330 million people coming together to share everything would require new, and impossible, logistics. Plus, how many of the 330 million people want to create? How many can create?

To the people who point to the Book of Acts or any type of socialist system in Europe, I say yea, you could fit 30 European countries inside of the continental United states. And in many of those bigger places in Europe and Asia where they've introduced socialism, it always morphs into some form of atheist communism, which rejects God all together.

Like I said, I've always been a capitalist. I led off this chapter with a quote from Milton Friedman who authored the book *Capitalism and Freedom* because I believe in the free market. My wife Angelike, who was raised by a single mother on welfare, is a perfect example of Friedman's quote, the free market raised her out of poverty. She and I are now the creators of products which we sell for profit and the fruit of our labor has changed the lineage of our family. God gave us specific gifts, or talents, and we've stewarded those accordingly, giving all honor to Him.

This book is based on developing your God-given gifts to produce something with Him and for his Kingdom. For example, I'm a Christain with a heart for writing and a heart for contribution but I have to sell this book to make a living and therefore, I can't give it away. It's both fair and Godly.

Now, if you purchased this book on a credit card, there's where we get into a different story. According to a 2021 WalletHub study, the average credit card interest rate was 18.26% for new offers. I offered this book at a fair price for my labor, but the credit card company charges you an astronomical interest rate, and that is usury as defined in the Old Testament.

All hard work brings a profit but mere talk leads only to poverty
Proverbs 14:23

For the third time, nowhere in scripture is debt viewed in a positive way. Knowing scripture and knowing God's purpose for your life and pursuing it, is critical to happiness. Who is missing God's word most according to the statistics? Young people. Who is socialism appealing to most? Young people. In a 2019 YouGov poll reported by Axios, 70 percent of millennials say they'd vote for a socialist. Nineteen percent of millennials and 12 percent of Gen Z said they thought the Communist Manifesto "better guarantees freedom and equality for all" than the Declaration of Independence.

If you know the track record of socialism and communism, that statistic is jaw dropping and should scare you. What our universities and senators fail to mention about these forms of government is that people still get very wealthy, only it's not private entrepreneurs, it's the government. The means of production is controlled by the state and carried out by the people who simply become a commodity. The biggest lie of the universities and senators is that these systems benefit the low income or middle class. In reality, the middle class actually disappears because these systems fail to honor the individual. They make promises in vain while the government (few) gets rich and the workers (people) become poor.

Just a strong opinion? Not at all. It's called the *income inequality gap* and according to Pew Research, the wealth gap between America's richest and poorest families more than doubled from 1989 to 2016. That's under the administrations of George Bush Sr, Bill Clinton, George W. Bush and Barack Obama, two Republicans and two Democrats. That's eye-opening. It's not a left or right thing, it's a rich (in Washington) control the purse strings thing.

True freedom, Biblical freedom, occurs when we free ourselves of debt and that takes responsibility. Young Americans between the ages of 18 and 29 owe more than one trillion dollars in student loans, mortgage and credit card debt. College graduates from the class of 2020 who took out student loans borrowed $29,927 on average, according to data reported to U.S. News in its annual survey. That's around $5,000 more than borrowers from the class of 2010 had to shoulder – representing a 20% increase in the amount students borrow.

That's both usury and deception. It's the same reason they bring you free drinks at the crap tables in Las Vegas. As long as you're ignorant of what's really going on, you'll keep repeating the same mistakes.

Remember the two rules of a fairy tale, the villains have something the protagonist, or main character doesn't (in this case money) and they know something they do not want you to know (in this case that the lending game is highly slanted in their favor.)

THE FINAL COUNTDOWN

I warn you, we're embarking on a dangerous time in history if we continue to miss biblical lessons surrounding work and money. I mince no words here, as my discernment around where we've been versus what lies ahead is crystal clear. Proverbs 12:24 clearly states *the lazy man will be put to forced labor.*

To me, there is no mistaking who the lazy man is in our day, it's the person who says I'm willing to do less if you promise to help me more. The current state of our union, meaning the prevailing trend of our government, is one which continues to promise entitlement and free things. It's the exact seduction of the enemy which mimics the kind of trap Eve fell into, surely you will not die, but you will have your eyes opened.

Precisely!

We're wooing young people with a distorted visual of socialism, placing rose-colored glasses on them and hiding history, literally. Those who teach it at the universities across the United States are like the serpent in the garden, giving only half truths, telling the young people they will not die, but they forget to tell them they will not fully live either.

MAN SAYS VS. GOD SAYS

Ambition has created the lightbulb, the car, the phone and the computer. The fruit of individuals pursuing their separate interests to improve the lives of ordinary people, that's free enterprise. What I hear more and more is to dream small, live in smaller houses, don't expect much and know that what you are doing is for the greater good. However, the Word of God is clear about using your gifts to turn profit, the parable of talents states that quite clearly. That's often the go-to story for most Christians who are in favor of the free market because it is quite obvious.

But consider this, Jacob, son of Issac, was rewarded for his what? Ambition. He desired the birthright. He esteemed to it. His brother Esau, on the other hand, failed to appreciate his birthright. He was rather lukewarm about it. Who was rewarded? Jacob. There is no mincing scripture here as it states there was something in the heart of Esau that repulsed God and something in the heart of Jacob that He loved (Malachi 1:2-3).

Do you desire to work for and move toward the Kingdom of Heaven or have you taken God's blessings for granted and turned your heart over to the musings of man? Caution, the hand of the diligent will rule, while the slothful will be put to forced labor. The Word clearly warns us to be careful, so if you are approached with a vote for an easy life, it's a ruse, a deception. God honors work. Ethical work.

"Whoever is lazy regarding his work is also a brother
to the master of destruction."
Proverbs 18:9

Once you've given up certain freedoms, God given freedoms, you are always put to work. The allure of an easy life, a carefree life with all the entitlements promised by the government, are so far from the teaching in the Word of God it's on another planet. Sloth is defined as a sin against God's love and is a dish served up by the enemy to entice and enslave an unsuspecting victim. Beware, what you eat today for free, you will pay dearly for in the future.

At times, I've referred to Christ's miracles, and have said, 'Well, Christ multiplied the fish and the loaves to feed the people. That is precisely what we want to do with the Revolution and socialism.
- Fidel Castro

The following statement was so shocking I had to verify it twice to make sure it was true. Fidel Castro was baptized into the Roman Catholic Church at the age of eight. He attended the privately funded

(Jesuit-run) Dolores School in Santiago. In 1945, Castro transferred to the (Jesuit-run) El Colegio de Belen in Havana.

Matthew 7:15 warns of this type of leader, telling us to *beware of false prophets, which come to you in sheep's clothing, but inwardly they are ravening wolves.* On record, there were a total of 95 minors that were killed by the order of Fidel Castro. Of these teens and children, 22 died by firing squad and 32 were killed in extrajudicial assassination. That's "on record," the numbers are much higher. Who knows how many others died in the ocean between Cuba and Florida attempting to escape Castro's savage dictatorship.

What did Castro multiply other than pain and suffering? Nothing except despair and death. He began with a popular theme - Hope. He multiplied hope and preyed on people's desire for change. That's what we're seeing now in a dangerous deja vu. That is why we've seen such a push to serenade young people into socialism, because they have good hearts and they desire to have hope. And anytime you have innocent hearts who lack truth and discernment, the enemy seeks to steal, kill and destroy.

Rafeal Cruz, the father of United States Senator Ted Cruz, who escaped communist Cuba at the age of 18, says *Socialism requires that government becomes your god.*

Cruz left the Catholic church at 18 and became a Protestant Preacher saying in an interview with the National Review, "*The people at the Bible study had a peace that I could not understand, this peace in the midst of trouble. I knew I needed to find that peace by finding Jesus Christ.*"

I share this story about Castro and his revolution because I grew up in South Florida where many of my closest friends, who were Cuban, were directly impacted by his diabolical deception, mincing politics and "religion" to twist scripture. History will always repeat itself as there are many right now at the highest levels of the United States government who claim Christianity as their foundation but fail to govern by its principles.

It's an important distinction that Jesus neither sided with Rome nor the Pharisees and the Sadducees. If we are to succeed, we are called to lead by his example, being cautious of any place where man can abuse his authority, be it in government or church. It's a tough assignment because we don't exist in a vacuum, but that is why being in pursuit of the Word is critical.

COMING IN FROM THE COLD

The cold war was about two things, economics and freedom. It appeared to be over when, on June 12, 1987, Ronald Reagan told Soviet leader Mikhail Gorbachev, "Mr. Gorbachev, tear down this (Berlin) wall." But what felt like an end now seems to be only a short reprieve. It's why the responsibility of every American who remembers that moment at the Brandenburg Gate in West Berlin, is to not fall back into deception. Test everything against the Word of God.

Just like blood flows, so does money. It has to circulate. The question though is this, has Christianity clouded or twisted its followers' views of what success means? Can a Christian living in

America today confidently say "I want to make more money and still rest their head on their pillow at night without feeling guilty?

I would answer that with an unequivocal yes! Most entrepreneurs I've encountered are creative and generous, they are bold and willing to put themselves out there for the sake of living an extraordinary life and risk is always part of the equation. Not everybody gets the same reward, not everybody gets a trophy.

If you are part of a system that rewards hard work and encourages the doubling and tripling of talents then you are living in Godly prosperity and money is indeed a part of that prosperity. What we do with our abilities and resources is to show our master that we are a good and faithful servant by treating our income as a source of life, to allow any financial fruit to act as a consecration to the Kingdom of God.

Ronald Reagan once said **"*The truth is, before entrepreneurs can take, they must give*"** and I believe giving is at the heart of every person who has a Bible on their desk or in their briefcase and seeks the authority of it, over the authority of man.

I AIN'T NO FORTUNATE SON

Do yourself a favor and go to some of the most popular politicians' Wikipedia pages and scroll down to *Early Life* and *Education*. You find a majority of the biggest names in public policy over the last decade have had ties to prestigious parochial educations at both the secondary and university levels, names like Trump, Biden, Pelosi,

Cuomo, Macron, Trudeau, Newsome, Fauci, Kerry and Clinton. Which of those names invokes the thought of biblical principles of governing?

The same earthly authorities who have the most dominion over us are the ones we hear every election cycle promising peace and prosperity. But isn't it interesting how income inequality continues to grow while violence, abortion and war continue to fill the headlines despite these beloved leaders promising differently.

Are we surprised?

The church I attended in South Florida as a child had a sign posted on the door that read "**Judas Left Early Too.**" To the parishioners this was just a friendly reminder to wait until mass was over before leaving. It was a clever way of saying "what's the rush?" Now that I think about it, it feels like we can use that sign again today on a grand, or worldly, scale as a reminder to those lawmakers who willingly deceive Jesus and turn on him for 30 pieces of silver (riches). They're the ones who've mastered the game, hiding the truth from us.

Each of those presidents and authority figures mentioned above claim to be believers but fail to legislate by the Word as if God will look upon them one day and say "well, it was your duty to country before Me I suppose." Not likely. That's not what it says in his book.

The allure of earthly riches and power lies at the heart of man's fall from grace. It's the great deception and why the Bible is about man's rejection of God and God's unending desire to restore that relationship, even those who seem most lost. Those are who my children remind me to pray for the most, they say "Daddy, don't forget, we must pray for their hearts to be overturned and restored." If the world were run by children, we might be better off I think.

There has to be accountability, not a reset, not *it's not your fault* or *what difference does it make?* The public school system, university system and government are failing to teach money principles and pretending to live by Godly principles at the same time.

"Therefore, say to the Israelites: 'I am the LORD, and I will bring you out from under the yoke of the Egyptians. I will free you from being slaves to them, and I will redeem you with an outstretched arm and with mighty acts of judgment
Exodus 6:6

It shouldn't surprise you that the same people who've been controlling Washington D.C. for the better part of the last 40 years are the same people who control financial aid and do stump speeches on entitlements and student loan forgiveness.

A dependent slave class from cradle to grave, that is what our children mean to those who hold earthly authority. The same leaders who love floating the idea of free stuff also cross their fingers behind their backs saying you'll pay much more with your freedoms, interest rates and taxes than you would have if you'd just saved and bought it yourself.

A peace in the midst of trouble, that is the Biblical definition of prosperity we learned from Jeremiah 29:11. There is a financial component to Biblical prosperity as well but it's up to us, the believer, to teach it, not our schools and not our government. It's not beneficial to earthly authority figures of the world to fix it, so they just keep pretending as if they are trying, the same way Judas kept pretending to be faithful to Jesus.

Proverbs 22:7 says *The rich rule over the poor, and the borrower is slave of the lender.* These days we look at the trillions being borrowed and spent as if it's Monopoly money. We can't even wrap our minds around it. This is what a trillion looks like 1,000,000,000,000. This is what the United States national debt clock looked like in the second of time I did a screenshot of it in April of 2022 when I wrote this paragraph: $30,360,794,025, 877.

It seems most people can look at that number and just say "wow" but not hold it personal. It's personal to me and should be for every parent in our country. I look at my three young girls and sigh. The last thing Angelike and I want to do is to allow their generation to inherit a country drowning in debt and enslaved to the government. Therefore we teach them about stewardship. We teach them how to make money, how to grow money and how quickly you can lose it if you're not careful. Most of all, we preach to them personal responsibility.

Clearly, usury is defined in scripture as *detestable*, yet we pay no attention to it. Debt is bad, yet we tolerate it. Interest is a form of enslavement, yet the majority of people walking the planet today buy into it. We aren't taught differently, so why would we? That is why we need to revive the WORD OF GOD. The answers are right there, in personal responsibility and hard work. It's clearly defined in the Bible, where God specifically tells his children to have multiple streams of income or diversity in your portfolio.

Ecclesiastes 11

Ship your grain across the sea; after
many days you may receive a return.
Invest in seven ventures, yes, in eight;

you do not know what disaster may come upon the land.
Sow your seed in the morning,
and at evening let your hands not be idle,
for you do not know which will succeed, whether this or that,
or whether both will do equally well.

Sounds a lot like advice one might get from the small gods of our time like Gary V, Tony Robbins or Robert Kiyosaki right? Here's the irony, these are the words of King Solomon, author of Ecclesiastes and the richest man who ever lived. They were authored by divine inspiration from God, as was King Solomon's most famous line "there is nothing new under the sun." In other words, the gurus of the 21st century can repackage the most reliable wisdom ever written, God's word, all they like, but the simple fact is, God said it first. It's been there all along. That is why to be in the pursuit of wisdom means to be in the pursuit of the Word.

WON'T GET FOOLED AGAIN

Here is where I have to tell you what I learned in my studies, that it's neither left nor right like the Bible says. The goal is not to be politically correct, but biblically correct and in a nation divided, such as ours, there doesn't seem to be room for dialogue, nobody willing to put their money where their mouth is and meet in the middle. Nobody who really says let's see what God's instructions are and get back to moral law. The love or lust for money is evil and has nothing to do with the system of capitalism as much as it does the nature of man.

The truth is both congress and colleges have been slowly edging out the authority of God. A perfect example of this is Harvard University. Founded in 1636 for the purpose of training Christian Ministers, it was named after Reverend John Harvard and its original motto was "In Christi Gloriam" which means "For the glory of Christ" in Latin. In 1836 it was changed to *Veritas Christo et Ecclesiae,* or "Truth for Christ and the Church." In 1880, Harvard eliminated Christ and the church in the seal, and since then, it's simply been *Veritas* or truth.

If you recall in chapter two, we don't just want answers, we want the truth! In our world we see this twisting of it, there's this truth and that truth, their truth and our truth and so we find ourselves in a watered down assembly of half truths.

Where is the truth springing from in our country if not from the Bible? May I suggest Harvard, it seems to be the mecca of truth for America, at least legally and legislatively.

Four twentieth century Presidents (Roosevelt, Kennedy, Bush (43) and Obama) all graduated from Harvard. That accounts for more than a quarter of the century as Roosevelt served three terms and Bush and Obama both served two. Of the current nine members on the Supreme Court, four (Neil Gorsuch, Stephen G. Breyer, Elena Kagan and Chief Justice John Roberts) attended Harvard. Ruth Bader Ginsburg, who served on the court from 1993 until her death in 2020 also attended Harvard Law. And finally of the 116th congress, Harvard Law by far surpassed all other schools with 23 members being alumni. The next closest was Georgetown (a Jesuit University) with 14.

Call me crazy, but with that much influence, I'd like to think the truth means Christ's truth. But one university, founded in faith, that took Christ out of its motto, is having a significant impact on everything happening in our country. I think it's worth mentioning as well that in 2021, Greg Epstein, an atheist and author of "*Good Without God*" was unanimously elected as Harvard's chaplain.

Prior to his election, Epstein was the Humanist Chaplain at the storied university where his focus was on teaching students about the progressive movement that center's on people's relationships with one another instead of God. That's what Humanism is, a philosophical stance that considers human beings *the starting point* for serious moral and philosophical inquiry.

This may be nothing, and I've even considered if these last couple of paragraphs deserved to be in the book, but I'm willing to go with my discernment on this as it pertains to everything about money and authority that has been mentioned here. And that is, if earthly authority keeps insisting on taking God out, we, as the Body of Christ, have to be more bold and insistent in putting God back in.... to everything we do.

That's free will.

DID YOU KNOW?

Let's revisit the Apostle Paul because he is that important. Our second look into his life lends itself to the validity of the Bible and that is; Paul would've been the last person preaching in favor of Jesus as, prior to his conversion, he took great offense to the claim that Jesus was the son of God. In fact he persecuted the followers of Jesus relentlessly.

But the man who once persecuted Christians would become a man who risked his life to save them. The following is critical to understanding Paul's absolute commitment to furthering the Gospel and spreading the teachings of Jesus.

Paul tells us in 2 Corinthians 11:24-26 *Five times I received from the Jews the forty lashes minus one. Three times I was beaten with rods, once I was pelted with stones, three times I was shipwrecked, I spent a night and a day in the open sea, I have been constantly on the move. I have been in danger from rivers, in danger from bandits, in danger from my fellow Jews, in danger from Gentiles; in danger in the city, in danger in the country, in danger at sea; and in danger from false believers.*

To doubt Paul, arguably the most instrumental figure in the preaching of Jesus' message, who penned 13 of the 27 books in the New Testament, is to doubt human nature. I find it tough to believe that a man would take one hundred and ninety five lashes on the back for a lie? A fabrication? Or even something he "kinda believed."

Would he do that?

Not just a lash, but a lash from a device specifically designed to break a man's will at all costs.

A Cat o'nine tails was a whip of nine chords with knotted balls on the end, designed to inflict massive amounts of pain. Paul received 39 lashes for his preaching about Jesus Christ not once, not twice, not three times, not four, but five times. At one point they carried his limp body outside as they thought he was dead.

So I ask you again, really? For a made up story? A half truth? How many lashes do you think you'd take for even a story you were 50/50 on? Not more than ten I'd predict before most mortal men would be like okay, it's really not that important. I'll be quiet and go home now.

It makes more sense to think only a man who saw a clear vision of Jesus and had his heart completely transformed would have such conviction.

Should we mention that he endured three shipwrecks and multiple imprisonments as well? Again, here is his answer as to why.

Why would I risk death and fight wild beasts? For nothing? To gain nothing? If there's no life after death why would I risk my own? Specifically what have I gained if the dead are not raised
1 Corinthians 15:32

CHAPTER 12

WHO YOU SAY I AM

You can analyze all you want, but you can never explain away
the God factor. Sometimes God just decides to breathe on
something and it's completely His prerogative.
- Brooke Fraser

Because we live in a culture where it seems money, politics and fame dominate our worldview, it's hard to see where we can fit God into our lives outside the scope of an hour at church on Sunday.

The Kingdom of God is tangible and each day when you put your feet on the floor, and see what's in front of you, that's an acknowledgment of creation itself. Something created that space you are standing on, and I'm not referring to the builder or carpenter who laid your tile or flooring, I'm talking about the builder of the earth beneath it and the carpenter who validated that creation by his life and death.

Whatever that place you stand on may look like for you at this point in your life, it's part of God's Kingdom and that is a truth that is being hidden from you. To reclaim that knowledge, it will take all of your senses to smell, taste, touch, hear and see. Accepting the invitation to create something meaningful in your home, business or community means to get back in touch with being human and to become more aware of what is artificial. Whether you cut hair, drive a truck, sell real estate or clean teeth, there's an opportunity to get more in tune with your creator and to help shift the world more inline with that which God originally intended. You just have to look for it. It's literally surrounding you but we've become desensitized to it in order that we fall asleep and become less aware of His wonders.

If you want to view paradise
Simply look around and view it
Anything you want to, do it
Want to change the world?
There's nothing to it

If these words sound familiar, you've probably seen the movie *Willy Wonka and the Chocolate Factory* and recognize the song *Pure Imagination*. In Colossians 3 it says **Let the message of Christ dwell among you richly as you teach and admonish one another with all wisdom through psalms, hymns, and songs from the Spirit, singing to God with gratitude in your hearts.** While Pure Imagination is neither a hymn nor worship song, I mention it because it brings back the child in me and reminds me, we need to acknowledge God's original plan, paradise, and we do need to change the world by co-creation with God again as our foundation. In order to better convey the spirit of creation, allow me to use one of the greatest gifts God gave to humans, the sense of hearing and, in particular, music. It speaks so much to the ruach as I described earlier, all that motives, stimulates, inspires and influences.

I love being a writer, but my heart belongs to music and while I love all genres, jazz is the most special to me because it's probably the closest thing I can think of to pure creation the way it's described in Genesis.

At first listen, it sounds like a formless void, almost chaotic. In fact, it turned me off initially. I thought "where is the genius in this? I don't get it." I can compare that to how I first viewed the Bible, thinking I don't see what others see. But one day in the middle of a song, there was suddenly a spark, and out of nothing came life and out of that life I saw beauty, I saw pure creation.

I feel like jazz touches the God gene and provides a wonderful metaphor for life in that often you must lose yourself and surrender before you can even remotely figure out how to create.

I believe evangelist D.L. Moody put it best when he said *"Before we pray that God would fill us, I believe we ought to pray for Him to empty us."*

That's the "letting go" part and it doesn't mean a clean slate in which you forget your past and start over, it means to give into the will of God and stop trying to white knuckle your way to prosperity. To be emptied means you now have more capacity to let the things that don't serve you out and, in turn, clear room to let the Holy Spirit in. When 100 executives tell me overwhelm is killing their ability to focus and create happiness, it's a sure signal to me that we're not meant to "be all" and "do all" even if technology affords us that opportunity.

There is a major difference between Self Development, which typically centers around strength through work, and God Development, which speaks of strength through grace. They both can be powerful but the first has a tendency to eat you up and the latter will always build you up.

Think of all the stress, the cortisol and the self sabotage that takes place simply because we're led to believe that the only way to achieve is via hustle. Right now, the world is struggling as a whole because so many of us are struggling in our own stories. Enter the Christian definition of grace - *the help given to us by God because God desires us to have it.*

God has a deep desire to help us, but it's hard for him to get through when your day is filled to capacity with gods (small g) who take up all of your bandwidth. Allowing God in to do his work and expanding your ability to create through grace is something I feel can be best explained via jazz.

"You have to play a long time to be able to play like yourself."
- Miles Davis

In 1983, the Top 100 Billboard charts were full of familiar names like The Police, David Bowie, Donna Summer, Styx, Hall & Oates and some guy named Michael Jackson. But despite all that starpower, it would be a former child prodigy who played Mozart's Piano Concerto No. 5 at the age of 11, who was about to revive his struggling jazz career and revolutionize music as we know it forever.

When Herbie Hancock's *Rockit* was released in June of '83 it was nothing short of groundbreaking, seen as the first recording in history to use synthesizers, scratching and sampling to cross all genres and bring hip hop to the mainstream. When Hancock performed it at the

1984 Grammy Awards, a majority of the 44 million viewers, watching Hancock and his keytar (keyboard guitar) in front of a DJ scratching, were seeing this new genre, this creation of man's imagination, for the first time.

But long before Rockit though, Hancock was a 23 year old protege to legendary jazz musician Miles Davis, a man he says taught him things that would have a profound impact on his music and his life.

"He told me whatever happens musically, you try to turn it into something of value and rather than be judgmental about what some other guy is playing, leave judgment out of the picture and just take what's there and make something happen with it."

In a busy overwhelmed world, what a great lesson on how to create something of value in our own lives. Jesus tells us that he didn't come to judge but to save and give life (John 3:17) and when I think about bringing that same philosophy to my life, I tell myself to stop getting distracted by judging myself and others and focus more on allowing myself to take what's available to me and make something out of it.

"That's not an easy thing to do," Hancock said in his 2006 documentary *Possibilities*. "It takes a lot of courage, a lot of trust and it takes a kind of nakedness."

Again, an interesting choice of words, nakedness. Where have we heard that before? In Genesis, God approaches Adam who was hiding from him and asks "who told you that you were naked?" The scripture symbolizes the loss of innocence as, for the first time, he and Eve are aware of being unclothed. We were created naked and were unaware. We were free in paradise and given dominion over all that was in it. I interpret this "nakedness" Hancock speaks of in the creation of the music process as a great lesson for any of us who wish to do the same in our profession.

I ask my clients all the time "who told you you couldn't do it?" meaning who said you should feel ashamed or embarrassed for being you? Hancock reminds me that you can't come into the fullness of what God created you to do without the courage and (God) confidence that says it's alright be naked (metaphorically speaking).

We water-down our capacity to create when we become hyper-sensitive to what our neighbors think and crave the validation of others, rather than that of God. It's why when we dream of being naked it indicates some type of vulnerability or self-consciousness. We want to hide as a defense mechanism to protect ourselves from judgment. But when we are reminded of who created us and what power is given to us, that is when we can release that fear and judgment and put an end to our insecurities.

Do not throw away your confidence; it will be richly rewarded.
You need to persevere so that when you have done the will of God,
you will receive what he has promised
Hebrews 10:35–36

Social media exacerbates this feeling of self-awareness as it can seem as if we're operating in a fishbowl at times. It certainly represents a drastic change from how we interacted and created wealth just 10 to 15 years ago. We're immersed in the language and images of a culture that craves instant validation and immediate feedback and that's just a tough place for the creative process to flourish because it keeps us under a certain amount of stress without a long game to judge our efforts by.

We spend so much energy worrying about who's watching us, attracting the right eyes, looking for the big break or connection that can change our brand or our love life in an instant, that we can easily forget the power of the one who sent us and what our true assignment is. Notice in the previous Hebrews scripture above how the word persevere is used, that indicates long game, not instant gratification or validation.

Real change and transformation doesn't come from pounding your chest or yelling out an affirmation, but rather from listening to God and knowing "I am who you say I am." I beg you not to get clouded in the allure to be loud and demonstrative, it's often the loudest influencers in entertainment and government, who have the weakest foundation behind the scenes. It's a straw house, or argument, they build with.

GET ON THE TRANE

In Isaiah, he hears the voice of the Lord asking, "Whom shall I send? Who will go for us?" Isaiah responds with a confident yes, saying "Here I am. Send me." Those five simple words could replace every affirmation you've ever made at a self-development seminar because you're now tapping into the supernatural power of the one who creates all things. Here I am, use me, is a contract between you and God that puts your business in the unique position to be His hands and feet in the marketplace.

As I mentioned earlier, we all possess an innate desire to be chosen. The Word of God reassures us, that when we say here I am, send me, there are no asterisks, there is no small print, God uses even the broken and when you say yes, He will most definitely reach down in the middle of your biggest mess and call you to serve.

John Coltrane was definitely broken. He was a gifted saxophone player who had the opportunity of a lifetime when he was asked to play with Davis in his quintet. In the jazz world it's like the equivalent of Tom Brady asking you to be his wide receiver. That was until one day when Davis caught Coltrane shooting heroin and fired him from the band on the spot.

As he lay in bed at home in Philadelphia shaking uncontrollably with cold sweats, his family would pass by and pray over him and he himself would ask God to give him one more chance.

Those prayers, and his willingness to surrender to God, helped him not only kick his demons cold turkey but in doing so He formed a relationship with his Creator that provided inspiration for his greatest work.

"I experienced, by the grace of God, a spiritual awakening which was to lead me to a richer, fuller, more productive life," Coltrane said.

Those words can be found in the liner notes of the album which he called his *thank you to God*, titled *A Love Supreme (1965)*. It's considered a masterpiece, ranked among Rolling Stone's 100 greatest albums of all time

Of particular note is that Coltrane recorded it in a single session on December 9, 1964, which tells me it was most definitely touched by a higher authority.

The liner notes continue; *"In gratitude, I humbly ask to be given the means and privilege to make others happy through music and that this album is a humble offering to Him, an attempt to say, Thank you, God. Through our work, even as we do through our hearts and with our tongues. May he help and strengthen all men in every good endeavor."*

The major takeaway here is that when you fully surrender, even in brokenness, at your darkest hours, you allow your gift to meet the will of the gift-giver, and that's when masterpieces are made.

There is one more critical takeaway from the Coltrane story that I simply couldn't avoid as it's extremely relative to our culture today.

In our desire to matter to the world and be fully known to God, sometimes we get the signals mixed up or become impatient so we start to copy somebody's voice, their brand or mannerisms in a counterfeit of creation where the "follower" becomes nothing more than a facsimile of somebody else.

This is best evidenced in a viral video by the rapper Snoop Dog that garnered over 27 million views on YouTube. In it, Snoop takes aim at the lack of originality that swept through the industry as he imitates a dozen of his contemporary rappers, essentially mocking them for how they all sound the same.

Be it hip hop, social media or business, the term duplication has become such a trending word in our culture that it's possible to miss the fact that God specifically speaks of multiplication, not duplication. In Genesis He said "be fruitful and multiply," he didn't say "be fruitful and duplicate." The nuances between the two nouns cannot be overlooked, to multiply is to increase in favor or in number whereas to duplicate is to create two identical parts the same as one another.

If we look to scripture, God made Adam first, and when it came time for Eve, his helper, He didn't duplicate man, because Adam was not incomplete. Eve was a compliment to him. The same way, either personally or professionally, if we look for somebody to plug holes in our bucket, it's the wrong approach. We look for partners in life, personally and professionally, not to *complete* us, but rather to <u>compliment</u> us. It's one thing to model steps, but steps apart from your Christ-centered individuality is where we get lost.

If we go back to Jazz, you'll have a hard time finding two artists or two songs that sound completely alike because the genre compliments individuality and one's ability to create in the spirit. Hancock said it's "all about being in the moment." Coltrane said you shouldn't even categorize him as jazz.

"Jazz is a word they use to sell our music, but to me that word does not exist...My music is the spiritual expression of what I am: my faith, my knowledge, my being. I just play John Coltrane."

Angelike and I have partnered with different companies but we never wanted to become them, to carry their flag or label over ours. We saw too many people lose their identity in a parent company. What we do, like Coltrane in some way, is as a spiritual expression of our intent to co-create with God. I hated labels like coach, influencer or network marketer, I just wanted to be David Norrie.

This is where, in our desire to create something or be somebody, we have to be willing to hover in the chaos and not just rush into making something cheap or incongruent for the sake of collaboration or making a quick buck.

It's easy to grow impatient and become afraid of falling behind because of "FOMO" especially when people call you and say "I've got an opportunity for you, but you have to act quickly." That can be a real tough "no" in a culture of "now." That doesn't mean it can't be simple, God does not complicate things. It means you have to have trust in the co-creation process and put it through the filter of the Word, knowing that if you listen and are obedient, the spark always comes. And when it comes, suddenly you have life.

SOMEBODY'S WATCHING ME

There is one more very important story about co-creation with God that my musical mind has to share.

One night while sitting with my family wondering what to watch, I came upon a video of opera singer Andre Bocelli. Immediately I was in awe of his voice and how effortless it seemed for him to hit all of those notes. "What a gift" I said to Angelike as I began thinking silently to myself, just once I'd love to do something that good, that powerful and that effortless.

As I began to watch a little more intentionally, it dawned on me, here is a blind man, standing alone on this massive stage in New York City with an enormous orchestra behind him. He stands completely still, visually unaware of his surroundings as he has just one job, to let it rip and unleash the gift God blessed him with in ultimate confidence.

What a powerful lesson, to watch a man go about his work

unable to judge his audience's reaction. He's not looking at the woman in the front row, he cannot see the violinist to his right or the sea of people extending in the distance, but he can feel them and with that he can lean in and just be in his gifting.

With that in mind, I ask you, what could you accomplish without fear of who was watching or judging you? We've built these personality prison cells so to speak with walls made of vanity and self consciousness that keep us from taking the breath of God and becoming who He made us to be. Every selfie has 10 that didn't make the cut. Every video has a dozen in which we didn't think we were perfect enough. With all that "pressure," we can easily forget that, like Bocelli, we are flawed by nature but we are perfect in purpose. Like Hancock, we have to accept a sort of nakedness in order to create.

Paul, who I've mentioned many times, is another example of purpose over perfection. We know that scripture says some called him a babbler, but the Bible says nothing of his physical appearance. However, in apocryphal texts (books outside of the Hebrew Bible), he's described as a man of small stature, with a bald head and crooked legs with eyebrows meeting over a hooked nose. And here we are, talking about his impact thousands of years after his death.

I know our culture rewards physical beauty, but true power resides more in our passion and posture than our outer appearance. When we focus our energy on the things we don't have, it doesn't serve us.

To circle back to Bocelli, the other thing I learned from watching him is that he wasn't born blind, but at the age of 12 was afflicted by degenerative glaucoma and he lost his sight. In one interview he is asked if he has any regrets in life and without a moment's hesitation he declares no, that this was his destiny, saying:

Whoever puts his life in the hands of the one who created it, who wants him, desires and loves him, puts their life in good hands.

In other words, let it rip.

WALK THIS WAY

The confidence to persevere in life when HOW seems a hundred feet tall is tough, especially when family, career and politics all gang up to overwhelm you. We struggle, we pivot, and we might even bang our head against the wall searching for answers.

HOW is God's favorite question because He knows the answer. Moses was an 80 year old stutterer when he *became* the one to lead the Israelites out of Egypt. Sarah was 90 when she *became* a mother. David was the youngest and the smallest of eight brothers when he *became* a giant slayer.

I'll stop you before you say "but" because you're probably already in denial thinking those are just Bible stories. Are they? Are you this far into this book and still willing to put God in a box by saying "but."

To truly believe, we have to be open to His supernatural power in our lives, right here in modern days. On a personal level, maybe you're asking Him HOW because somebody told you that your *best days are behind you* or because you feel totally *alone in your assignment as a parent or in looking for true love*. Perhaps HOW permeates your business mindset because friends, or even family, have convinced you that *you don't possess the gifts to be who you dream of becoming* or that *your past is too littered with brokenness and mistakes* to start over. Or maybe HOW is just something you've grown accustomed to asking yourself because you set *goals that you feel are too big for you to tackle.* Regardless of what, they all have one thing in common - deception. Doubt in God and his supernatural ability to create significant change in your life is nothing more than an attack on you from the enemy of your soul.

Don't forget, the devil is perfectly happy with you just going through the motions, taking the path of least resistance and continuing to push your grand ideas off further into the future. His job is easy when all he has to do is whisper in your ear, confirming negative thoughts you already allowed in your head. He's good with you bowing to counter culture and playing along with the rules of society because he'd love nothing more than for you to be an unknowing soldier in his war to subdue the earth.

When you fail to fix yourself, you stop being a part of the solution to fix the world and this kind of attack on the individual is why, on a global scale, the enemy is saying "your God is losing and the way of life you've come to know and love, the things you cherish, the values you hold, the hope you had for your children, they're all gone now. Give up, the future is bleak."

How do we fight back and get a clear word from God as to HOW to proceed? Because if you are anything like me, you wake each day and ask "God, HOW did I get to this point?" "HOW am I supposed to lead my family during this crisis?" "HOW can I succeed in my vocation amongst the cut-throat competition out there?"

The first thing is, you gotta lean into it. I think most of the time we wanna run from overwhelming thoughts of HOW. We as humans are too quick to escape painful thoughts about our reality. Can't sleep – take a pill. Stressed out – take a drink. Bored – look at your phone. Can't create - copy somebody else. But when the goal is just to escape discomfort as soon as possible, you never really address the root feelings and therefore you rush into bad decisions.

Sometimes it's in the hovering or it's in the void, the discomfort of a season where we can clearly see what we are called to be and what we have to become in order to get there.

"The Lord directs the steps of the godly. He delights in every detail of their lives. Though they stumble, they will never fall, for the Lord holds them by the hand."
Psalm 37:23-24

I gain great strength from the Psalm above however, in my experience I've seen too many people take it out of context. God is clear, He delights in every detail but it doesn't say He directs every detail. As I've said over and over, He is not a micromanager.

Just like my daughter, I can direct her steps and point her in the right direction. I can delight in every detail, both victories and tough learning lessons. I'm there to hold her hand all the way and catch her from falling, but she still has to walk on her own.

Angelike and I teach this in what we call *The Turned On Method*, where we talk of a divine order and that through his Word we have a framework for wisdom, we have a framework for how to live, we have a framework for how to use discernment, but we still have to discover what He called us to be by leaning into Him and being obedient, even when times are rough and/or uncertain.

Sometimes He will call you to a place so much higher and into something so outlandish that you doubt endlessly that you can do it, yet you feel called to it. But that's God, and when you trust Him, and are obedient to Him, the glory becomes all His. Not by your strength and knowledge but your obedience and willingness to turn it all over to full time faith. Even when you ask for the next step and it is not quite clear. Even when you're in the middle of the fight and you feel like you're not winning, you have to accept grace in knowing that He is indeed moving pieces in your favor, it's just not so obvious in real time.

LISTEN TO YOUR HEART

At times when I was writing this book, my youngest was listening to the Baby Shark song on repeat, my two older girls were each watching their teacher homeschool them on the computer, Angelike was on calls for our business and Elvis, our dog, was busy barking at everybody who passed the window. The only thing I could compare it to was trying to do a calculus test at a rock concert. I couldn't hear myself think.

That's life for most people these days, we haven't got the time or the personal sanctuary to hear ourselves think, let alone be a place where God can talk to us. Don't forget, we're in concrete jungles where the last thing that resembles creation is the fake plant in the corner of the room.

As I was wrapping up the final edits, we found ourselves two blocks from the ocean in Santa Rosa Beach, Florida. On quiet nights I could hear the waves crashing and feel the breeze on my face and what do you know, God whispered to me then. I was in his presence, free of distraction.

What He tells us in the moments where we make space for Him impacts our lives more than we can imagine. The big opportunities for His favor are about presence and saying yes.

What about Simon Peter, a fisherman struggling to catch fish? Jesus calls out to him, like he whispers to us, and says Peter, you're working in your gift, but you haven't married your gift with my Father's calling yet. Don't worry, you're still gonna fish, only you'll use your talents for my Kingdom, and you'll be a fisher of men.

Peter didn't sit and wait. He got off the boat and went. Now granted he had a pretty awesome sign, I know, but we don't have to see Jesus to feel him and this is where some good people get caught up, sitting and waiting for a huge sign or for God to move chess pieces, when the nudge is there and they know it. Lingering in a place that you're supposed to be passing through is not good as we will find out.

If you can ever get quiet, at some point in your life you're going to listen for a calling and then respond in a leap of faith.

There will be times when you're under fire or when you can't see what's happening and all you know is, there doesn't seem to be much fruit or in Peter's case, fish. Those are the time when you lean in harder.

Laurie Beth Jones, author of Jesus CEO says "If you have not been tested by fire, you do not know who you are." Remember this, only after Jesus was baptized in the spirit and tested in the wilderness did he begin to fill in his "I Am" statements, meaning He said "I am the gate for the sheep." "I am the bread of life." "The light of the world." "I am the true vine." I am the Alpha and the Omega."

I AM, the two most powerful words in the English language. That's where we start to win, when we hold that hand up and say "here I AM."

I AM what though? Whatever follows these two words holds a great deal of weight and the problem I've seen is that too many people fill in that blank by regurgitating some ambiguous cliches they heard in self development circles. I AM authentic, dynamic, motivated, confident, kind, ambitious, fun-loving, unstoppable, abundant, unselfish,... etcetera, etcetera, etcetera...All of which are fantastic, but do they truly mean anything? Anything you'd want carved into your headstone?

No, these are the vague descriptions we often find in one's obituary. Stephen was a kind, unselfish man who owned his truth. Catherine was a charming wife and affectionate mother who stepped into her power.

This can be touchy here so forgive me. There is no sin in saying these things, I'm just asking if they bear fruit or if they lose their power when fear takes over and they simply become what they are, made-up affirmations.

When you speak God's Word over your life, it takes more than platitudes. I AM becomes something you wake up to each day and people begin to see that in your posture and actions. As you begin to do this, let me help by reminding you of something Pastor Tony Evans said; ***"If you were to ask yourself who you are, could you say it without giving your name, your occupation, your title at work or any*** *other of the obvious means we use to identify ourselves?"*

Here I am, Lord. I am on a mission to bring light to dark places. I am the head of my family. I am a man who will not allow culture to curb my enthusiasm for the Word. Here I am, I am your servant God because as for me and my house, we will serve the Lord.

Promise yourself this, whatever follows your "I AM," don't put it on the back burner for too long because after a while "I AM" becomes "I WILL" and then "I SHOULD'VE" and the present is lost. That is the safest and most gradual road to hell.

HAYAH

We now start, not by forming a new you, not by making you a copy of somebody else or even reinventing you, but rather by reviving the you God originally made in order to get your spark, or ruach, back. To do that, we begin with one very important and powerful word, *Hayah*, a verb in the original Hebrew text of the Old Testament which means to arise, to happen or become.

Hayah signifies what isn't, but now is, or what wasn't but has become. It is a beautiful word of creation and that is why it occurs most often in Genesis, the beginning. The earth was in a state of chaos and became something. Adam was not a living soul, he became one. A man shall leave his father and his mother and be joined to his wife; and they shall hayah (become) one flesh.

How does this factor into your story? Great question, and we start to answer that by contrasting where you are currently (actual self) with what you strive to become (ideal self). To become something that you *aren't yet, but are designed to be,* first requires attention, then the intention and finally the decision to follow through, that means to invite God into the heart of your journey.

Think about this, God rewards action and even when you don't make a choice, you're still choosing. What that means is that everything will become something, the question is will it become greater or lesser. When we invite God into our everyday lives, He helps us become the fullness of what we were intended to be. His is the partnership, which I've mentioned prior, where knowledge and unconditional love merge to achieve real transformation. It's the reason why, if you have failed to become "the something" you desired in the past, this time promises to be different.

To the contrary, if things are left alone, without an intelligent influence, without love and nurturing, they don't just stay static, but they deteriorate. For example, if you leave your garden alone it will become a weed patch or if you leave your pool alone it will become a cesspool of algae. If you neglect your children, are they more likely to become something magnificent or to deteriorate? If you don't touch your business will you create more wealth or will it regress?

To put it simply, life requires input and we have to be in pursuit of ways to grow everything we touch. Time has proven, even in the most desperate of cases, that the best way to become something greater and have a positive touch is through the Word.

Hayah is only used in scripture when God wants to express a dynamic existence, not static. I am David Norrie is static, that doesn't change, but I am becoming *Turned On* by means of being in *The Pursuit,* that is dynamic and a direct result of Angelike and I trusting in God's ability to provide direction and then taking action to meet

Him halfway.

Every time we seek to grow and become something new or better, we hayah. Can you guess after Genesis where the most occurrences for Hayah are found in scripture? In the books of Ezekiel and Jeremiah, the two prophets who existed during the most trying times in Israel's history, which directly relates to our circumstances now. The Body of Christ needs co-creation. We need to become something greater to change the world, so we look for the Holy Spirit to intercede on our behalf to make us strong. For you, that may look like becoming a better mother, father, husband or wife. In our professional lives we need the dynamic creation of ideas and wealth where there was once lack and poverty.

> *Fear you don't own me. There ain't no room in this story*
> *and I ain't got time for you telling me what I am not.*
> *- Francesca Battistelli*

In order to become something, we must also set aside the fear or doubt that we won't. Have you ever seen an interview with a top level athlete who says something to the effect of *there was never a time when I doubted myself, where I thought I wouldn't make it.*

Passage after passage in the New Testament we witness Paul having to fight fear and press on, speaking with consistency and conviction. There are no would'a, could'a or should'a from him, which is why his letters to the churches give us so much of what we need to build our spiritual muscle with. Paul never left room for maybes, he punctuated his sentences with periods and exclamation points. And just as we often speak to unwilling or contentious audiences during our days, his were often hostile and mocking. He says:

Why would I risk death and fight wild beasts?
For nothing? To gain nothing?
If there's no life after death why would I risk my own?
Specifically what have I gained if the dead are not raised
1 Corinthians 15:32

In the scripture above Paul was not literally referring to fighting wild beasts. No, one scholar said *this should be understood as a reference to evil spirits or 'beasts', at work in the demon-possessed, sorcerers, and idolaters of the city.*

Those heralding the Word of God could say the same about today's school boards, city councils, pop culture icons and new age idolaters. If we cannot become something greater and speak up in order to teach the Word with bold confidence, then the Word is in danger of being swallowed up by the cultural beasts that threaten it on a daily basis.

Once again, I'll point you to the words of A.W. Tozer who said;

"I'm not afraid of the devil. The devil can handle me – he's got judo I never heard of. But he can't handle the One to whom I'm joined; he can't handle the One to whom I'm united; he can't handle the One whose nature dwells in my nature."

Receive that! The one we are *united* with, the one whose nature dwells in our nature. Take that to the office with you each day and see what happens. Tell that to yourself before you get on your next sales call or lead your next team meeting.

What will you become through the desire to say here I am God, let's create. Because the longer you put it off and toil in mediocrity, kicking the can down the road again, promising yourself that one day you'll make a move, the longer you will remain in your own personal hell. Instead of "one day" we must re-order those words back into their order to "day one" and just be, just begin, just become... hayah.

RUNNING TO STAND STILL
Jonah, Joshua and Joash

There is a common thread that applies to every single person who desires to become something greater - You either open your heart and embrace the pursuit of God's assignment through His Word, or you don't.

Free will. I know, I've pounded that message into your head enough haven't I?

What I find really attractive about the Bible is that it's real, it's not just a bunch of kumbaya, everything ends perfectly, everybody is happy fairytale-type stories. It reflects life in every way. Some stories end in victory and others end poorly. As we get older and the clock starts ticking, you'll ask yourself, do I have another run in me, can I revive this body, this job or this relationship.

I believe we all get second opportunities and here is where we get more specific and narrow it down to three main stories of the Bible that will encompass every struggle you have with finding prosperity and, if you pay attention closely, they will definitely lead you to victory.

Jonah, Joshua and Joash. You don't have to be a biblical scholar to easily identify with their situations and to see your story in their stories. I boldly say that in the heaviest and most important parts of your life right now, you are either running from something, lingering in a place you were supposed to be passing through or simply not trusting God enough to give the full effort you need to win your battle.

Jonah ran. Joshua waited. Joash was lackadaisical. These are the three ways we can sabotage God's success plan for us. By studying these three Bible stories and applying them in your life, you will have Godly instructions on how to move mountains and pursue prosperity with a foundational wisdom of timeless proportions .

DID YOU KNOW?

The human eye is made up over over 2 million working parts. The optic nerve contains more than one million nerve cells and your eye can distinguish approximately 10 million different colors. The iris has 256 unique characteristics compared to your fingerprint which has just 40. A team of neuroscientists from MIT has found that the human brain can process entire images that the eye sees for as little as 13 milliseconds.

In the sixth chapter of *On The Origin of Species*, by Charles Darwin (November 1859), the famed scientists writes: **To suppose that the eye with all its inimitable contrivances for adjusting the** *focus to different distances, for admitting different amounts of light, and for the correction of spherical and chromatic aberration, could have been formed by natural selection, seems, I freely confess, absurd in the highest degree.*

I agree, but this is where many Christians stop, without giving further context to what Darwin continued with, also writing; **Reason tells me, that if numerous gradations from a simple and imperfect eye to one complex and perfect can be shown to exist, each grade being useful to its possessor, as is certainly the case; if further, the eye ever varies and the variations be inherited, as is likewise certainly the case; and if such variations should be useful to any animal under changing conditions of life, then the difficulty of believing that a perfect and complex eye could be formed by natural selection, though insuperable by our imagination, should not be considered as subversive of the theory.**

So maybe there is a chance this amazing creation known as the eyeball evolved to what we know is as today?

Nicolas Léonard Sadi Carnot (1796 – 1832) was a French physicist who is considered to be the "father of thermodynamics." Shortly after his death, around 1850, the German physicist Rudolf Clausius and the British born William Thomson (Kelvin), stated the basic ideas of the second law of thermodynamics and in 1865 introduced the concept of entropy.

Why does this matter?

Well, the first law of thermodynamics states that energy is constant; it can be transformed from one form to another, but can be neither created nor destroyed, neither increasing nor decreasing. If no natural process can create or destroy energy, then neither the universe nor the laws of physics can explain the existence of energy. This begs the question, how was the universe created? The most reasonable explanation is that something, or someone, outside of the laws of physics, and outside of the universe (God) created it.

The second law of thermodynamics involves a concept known as *entropy; the increase in the disorganization within a system.* In simple terms, it states that things will go from being organized into chaos. If the universe was infinitely old, it would now be in a state of maximum entropy (total chaos) and it wouldn't make sense that life would evolve from simple to complex because this second law indicates just the opposite.

The evolution theory claims that every physical system is the result of a spontaneous process of assembly. Such progression would be in complete violation of the second law of thermodynamics that says things tend to move to disorder where entropy.

CHAPTER 13

RUNNING FROM PROSPERITY

Men run from God as a creator, not because they don't like the idea that God created them but they don't like the idea that God is their judge.

It is perhaps the most common way human beings avoid happiness. We run from it.

How, you ask? Let me see, we run from responsibility, we run from commitment, we run from love, we run from confrontation and we run from having to grow up. Regardless of what we are running from, one thing is for sure, things eventually catch up to us and one day, whether we like it or not, we have to stop running and face these issues head on.

This is a story about Jonah. He was a runner. One of the all time greats in fact. Of the three Js, I use this one first for two reasons. First, I think the world is full of Jonahs right now, people running from God and his assignment for them. And second, it's very personal to me because I initially ran from the one thing that's blessed my life more than anything, my wife Angelike. And as you'll read, there is no doubt in my mind that God's hand was in it. So I can unequivocally say, and without the slightest embellishment, that were it not for my running like Jonah, then you would not be reading this right now.

YOU'RE GOING
THE WRONG WAY

If you haven't noticed, we're a nation on the move. We're all on a road to somewhere, trying to get home, longing for a place where we feel safe and comfortable. Speaking of being on the road, if you've ever watched the movie Planes, Trains and Automobiles, you probably can recall the scene when Steve Martin's character falls asleep in the passenger seat of the car and across the highway is another vehicle incessantly honking and yelling to John Candy "You're going the wrong way." Martin wakes up and inquires with "He says we're going the wrong way." Candy replies "He's just drunk, how would he know where we're going?"

The two men quickly find out the man's warning was right, they were going the wrong way, and they narrowly escape death, sandwiched between two semi trucks coming straight at them.

Before we dive into the heaviness of Jonah, I thought we might warm up with this light-hearted comic scenario because there are a lot of people telling us we're headed in the wrong direction these days. Do we brush it off, ignore them and continue on wondering how they would know where we're headed? The parallels are the same. We've both fallen asleep at the wheel and gotten comfortable in taking our eyes off the road (God) and becoming prideful when anybody tries to point this out. How would they (Biblical authors) know where we're going (we've evolved) so let's ignore the warnings.

Now Jonah loved God, but he was comfortable and very prideful so when God enlisted him to go to the city of Nineveh to preach a message of repentance to the people there, Jonah did just the opposite and ran off in the wrong direction. His reason? He despised the people of Nineveh. They were his enemy and therefore he felt they were beyond salvation. In fact, he'd rather God do just the opposite and destroy the city and its people, rather than save it.

This is a good teaching moment in the story as sometimes we are tasked with doing things which are difficult, things we'd just as well leave alone. Surely there might have been a time over the last couple of years when you were asked to talk to a friend, relative or business associate about something that you disagreed on and you said "nah, I'm good. You do you. I'll be over here, doing me." And you thought, they get what they deserve. Sounds like a popular phrase of our culture doesn't it? Maybe it was placed on your spirit to help a relative you weren't on speaking terms with or tell a friend they were going the wrong way in terms of their destructive lifestyle and instead you ran because it wasn't beneficial to you and you really didn't care for them anyway. So be it.

Certainly we see this disposition in our modern political climate, one side would rather see the other crash and burn, even at the expense of the country, rather than turn around and work something out to save the country. The left is literally rooting for the right to fail and vice versa. For what? So one can say they were right and the other was wrong. It's pride personified.

Jonah turns his back on God and hops on a merchant boat headed to the city of Joppa. This is where he shows us another flaw of human nature, escapism. He promptly goes below deck and falls asleep. First there was the turning away and now the avoidance or hiding. Try to relate. It's never just running from that which is difficult, it's the escaping and willful distraction that accompanies it.

This is where it gets personal for me. I'd been a bachelor all my life and at 37 years of age God placed an assignment on me in the form of marriage. Now unlike Jonah, I didn't run because I hated my assignment, I loved Angelike, yet still I ran. Why? Because I was scared. I got cold feet. So remember, there's more than one reason why we run.

In the spirit of self sabotage, I conjured up a pretty good fight with her over something immature and egotistical and then I literally fled, walking out the door in anger. I walked for miles in the opposite direction and instead of a boat, I hid out in a movie theater. Jonah distracted himself with sleep and I watched the movie Grown Ups (the irony of that title can't be lost). I was a boy still who needed to grow up.

As Jonah's story goes, he was awoken from his sleep by the sailors who said there's a massive storm and were inquiring what he had done to upset the gods, as they were pagans. In his humility, Jonah instructed the sailors to throw him into the ocean. They did, and the storm subsided. As he sank deeper and deeper, just before he could give himself up to the depths of the sea, a huge fish swallowed him up.

I AIN'T TOO PROUD TO BEG

Think for a moment about what it would be like in the belly of a whale, the stench and discomfort. Now think about what you are running from and how it swallows you up, the stench of pride and discomfort that keeps you hostage. When the spirit of pride takes over, we convince ourselves that we'd rather die (spiritual death) than to humble ourselves and face what needs to be faced. In my case, prosperity in the form of love was right there in front of me and I bolted.

Again, there are many reasons why we run, but why isn't the most important lesson here. I ran because I was scared of change and commitment. Jonah ran because he was full of judgment and animosity. It's the reasons we hide, the reasons why we choose to sedate or distract ourselves from the realities of life, which are the most important. If fear is the main reason behind running from God's assignment, I'd argue that stubbornness and pride are two of the main adjectives that describe a runner. You see fear, we can understand, fear is forgivable. But stubbornness and pride, two very dangerous strongholds, they are less about instinct and more about a cognitive decision to ignore God's will. They are the sins which keep us from turning around and facing what we need to face.

We must come to the realization that wanting to run is normal, but turning around and doing what's right needs to be normalized as well. It's a huge part of self development that speakers charge thousands of dollars to learn in their courses, but a lesson we'd know if we sought God's council first.

There are parts of your life, right now, which are suffering because of your unwillingness to turn around and have a difficult conversation. Parts of your life God is giving you a second chance to correct but you're still choosing to run and hide.

CHECK YOURSELF BEFORE YOU WRECK YOURSELF

Jonah was a miserable wreck inside of that whale. He was disobedient and rebellious. You're not going to believe this, but it was exactly three days I was miserable, disobedient and rebellious as well. I wrestled with God in prayer, just like Jonah did inside the belly of the whale. He told me to pick up the phone and call Angelike. This is the part where I'd like to say I was the hero of this story, and obeyed him, but I didn't. I was worse than Jonah, my pride and stubbornness were even greater than his. In fact, it was so strong that I was willing to drown in what I knew was a lifetime of regret and heartache rather than show humility and turn around.

Beat that for stubborn pride will ya.

> *...and the Lord commanded the fish,*
> *and it vomited Jonah onto dry land.*
> *(Jonah 2:10).*

In his leadership Bible, John C. Maxwell says *God gave Jonah a motive check*. When you find yourself in a bad place, you better check your motives, are they selfish or Godly? When my phone rang on that third evening and Angelike asked me to come over and talk, it was my second chance. Isn't it good to know we serve a God of second chances?

When I arrived at her house, the engagement ring I'd given her was on the table. It was just months before our wedding night, the invitations had already been sent out. Angelike took my hand, looked me in the eyes and said "David, before you walk out of the door for good, would you be open to reading the Bible with me for ten minutes?"

Remember, God never forces us, we have free will, so when love beckons, He never violates that, we have to make the decision on our own. It's a true testament of his character. He desires to overturn our heart and point us toward victory even when we run, even when we're stubborn, because he knows what's best for us.

I struggled with not knowing what to do and always wanting to be in charge. I was an impatient man who never had the time to open God's word. But that night, for the first time, my heart softened and I opened the Bible and read it with Angelike.

Sure I'd seen one before. Sure I'd heard it read in church, but I'd never opened my heart to it. More importantly, this was the first time anybody ever tried to translate it and put into context the words in that big, old, ancient book that I thought had no practical value in my modern life.

Knowledge teaching (Biblical wisdom) in conjunction with love (Angelike's love) led to my transformation. That day I became (hayah) something new, a true believer in Christ. Everything in my life changed in an instant. The scales fell off my eyes and I could see. I didn't ask for that and I can't explain it, but that's what happened.

Angelike's humility in calling me, combined with her boldness in putting her ring on the table, superseded my stubbornness and got me to break down my walls. Angelike and God co-created something that day.

In discussing this chapter of the book with her, she reminded me of a very important part of the story that I'll share with you here. She said;

"You were stubborn and if I thought I could win you back or transform your attitude on my own, I could've done it with sex, I could've done it by manipulation or I simply could've allowed you to walk all over me. But thankfully, I was mature enough spiritually to know that I couldn't convict you with my flesh or by myself, I knew you had to be convicted personally by Christ and the only way I was going to reach you was with his Word."

Angelike was right. It was the only way. Here I am a decade later and I look at the fruit that was produced from that one event where we both were obedient to God. Out of Angelike's courage and faith, and my willingness to surrender has come three beautiful children, the baptizing of both of my parents and a half dozen friends, millions of dollars in income, and now this second book to glorify God.

How to we fix the world? By fixing ourselves!

SAD SONGS SAY SO MUCH

My story has a happy ending, Jonah's not so much. It's scripture, not a fairy tale, with God as the author, giving us the rest of the story. Yes, Jonah goes to Nineveh and completes his assignment with the king and his people repenting after hearing his message. But where my story and his differ is that I let my emotions go and had a true transformation of the heart. To this day, no matter how much I'm tempted to go back to my stubborn stronghold, I always yield to God's call to humble myself and love my wife like Christ loves the Chruch. I turn around and face the difficult conversations even when instinct tells me to run. It's a foundation we've built our marriage on and trust me, we've had many tough conversations since that first one.

Jonah however never acquiesced to his emotions. He went back to his pride and stubborn ways, holding on to his indignation and pleading with God to kill him because he couldn't let his disdain for the Ninevites go. He couldn't stand to see them happy. The last we hear of Jonah is him sitting under the hot sun telling God he'd wished he were dead.

I don't have to try hard to get you to realize how important this book of the Bible is to our world right now. Can you imagine getting a word from God in this political climate to give to your enemy to spare them from his wrath? You might be like Jonah and say *why should I? They're not Godly like me so why not let them perish?*

This should smack us in the face and remind us, winning an election doesn't solve our problems if there is no change of heart. If we just go back to our separate corners and wallow in hate, there is no real winner, it only perpetuates more hate and jeopardizes furutre generations. Elections don't soften hearts, the Lord does. Presidents and Senators don't have the final say, God does.

If we could only see through the eyes of a child. My girls always remind me not to scorn my enemies but rather to pray for a turning over of their heart. Even at their tender ages, they know forgiveness is possible when you listen to God's instructions.

FIGHT OR FLIGHT?

Staying positive these days is tough. Whether you're constantly battling the chatter in your mind or trying to close the door on something from the past, it's hard to be your own motivational coach on a daily basis. Sometimes you have to go into the belly of the whale and wait it out. The belly of a fish paints a clear picture of an uncomfortable place to wait. Life is going to be uncomfortable at times, and that's why we escape. We escape via scrolling social media, abusing alcohol or drugs or we simply escape in a den of pride. It's all a diversion of the enemy. He'd like nothing more than for you to keep running rather than turn and seek resolution with the help of the Lord.

If you desire to make a turn in the right direction and reconcile with a loved one or with God, then realize, the decision is tough but the action may be even tougher. In scripture, David ran from King Saul who repeatedly tried to kill him, but David gathered the courage to turn around and confront him. He could've killed Saul but instead *David bowed down and prostrated himself.* They talked it out, David having penetrated Saul's heart much the same way Angelike did mine. Saul said *You are more righteous than I... You have treated me well, but I have treated you badly.*

Again, we're given a compelling example as to the power of words when combined with courage and humility.

Escapism is becoming a major theme of our culture, and with more political polarization and more virtual places to escape to, there will never be a shortage of boats to hop on. We're making running and quitting easy. In the chapter on money, I mentioned how quitting on debt and running away from financial responsibility is now something our government official's stump for at every microphone. That's not God's law. It's man's.

In the Bible we're given example after example of instances of adversity and none of them encourage escape, instead they deliver a clear message that avoidance and running must be met with courage and confrontation.

Running is often a natural instinct, so don't beat yourself up if you've done it or if you're doing it right now. It doesn't mean you're weak or bad. It's how you resolve the situation when you get that motive check that matters. When God gives you that second chance, you go to battle.

If it's fear that's causing you to run, turn around and face it. If pride is a roadblock, be like Angelike, stubborn to please in the eyes of the Lord and willing to fight and put what you believe on the line when your spirit tells you to. Be a knowledge teacher, strong and unwavering but be a love teacher too, forgiving and eager to reconcile. That's where transformation occurs.

It's time to stop running from people or things in our lives that make us uncomfortable. God's word is clearly telling us to go back to and correct things, to finish our assignment, so we can say we've run our race to completion.

DID YOU KNOW?

The story of Jonah is very real.

A major issue some people have with the Jonah story is, they ask are we supposed to take it literally? Surely, you don't expect us to believe a man can live in the belly of a whale for three days do you?

The Bible is so beautifully constructed and perfect in purpose and this is one of those things its detractors love to shine a light on as "impossible." I get it, that's understandable. First, we know Jesus used parables for some of his most important teachings. Second, allegories in the Bible are always identified as such and Jonah's story shows no signs of that. Third, Jonah was a real man; Jewish, Christian and Muslim scriptures all speak of the prophet Jonah. While some brush off the story as satire or fictional, I believe that a God who created the universe and everything in it is, by definition, a supernatural God and would absolutely be able to create an experience such as Jonah's.

Most notable though is that Jesus himself confirms the story saying ***"For as Jonah was three days and three nights in the whale's belly so shall the Son of man be three days and three nights in the heart of the Earth."*** *Matthew 12:40*

Furthermore Nineveh, where Jonah was sent, is historically accurate as an ancient city, which archeological records prove worshiped a fish-god called Dagan. Perhaps that is why upon being spit out, Jonah had to say so little in order to get the people there to repent. Perhaps God used a fish to strengthen the message He tasked Jonah with, which is one of repentance. Regardless, the tale of Jonah is not so much about sitting in the belly of a fish but rather its importance lies in the fact that we can't run from our assignment.

CHAPTER 14

SHOULD I STAY OR SHOULD I GO

You Can't Inhabit Canaan
With an Egypt Mindset

When Angelike and I sat in the auditorium that day, I had no idea what to expect. I had known the speaker, Scott Rigsby, for a couple years having interviewed him for a piece I wrote on Triathlons, but this would be the first time I was in the audience to hear him speak.

It would be a moment of lasting impact in my faith journey.

The first words out of his mouth were *"if you came here today to hear my story, then you are going to be sadly disappointed. My story is filled with pain, sorrow, and great disappointment. It's a story about a young man drowning in a sea of despair. But what you will hear today is God's story, my role in it, and how I built a life in the services of others."*

Twenty-two years prior to that moment, Rigsby was a 18 year old young man who's second home became an Atlanta trauma hospital where medical professionals were trying to save his left leg. He'd already lost the lower right one in a horrific auto accident involving a tractor trailer that almost took his life.

Having battled the demons of depression, anger, resentment, pity and grief, all while self medicating and suffocating in quiet desperation, one day God gave him what he says was a "burning bush" moment when He told him to run an Ironman race. But not just any Ironman, the legendary Ironman World Championship in Kona, Hawaii.

Rigsby was 20 years past his prime and out of shape. Even worse, he was financially strapped and working a dead end job. He didn't know how to swim without legs, had never ridden one of those fancy triathlon bikes, and had not even come close to running a fraction of the 26.2 miles required for the brutal endurance race. If all that wasn't challenging enough, he was also dealing with a traumatic brain injury sustained in his accident that caused him to suffer from narcolepsy.

Despite those obstacles, one year and 10 months later, just before midnight, Rigsby would cross the finish line in Hawaii and become the world's first double amputee with prosthetics to finish the Ironman World Championship.

WHAT'S LEFT OF ME

The medical term for what's left of a limb after an amputation is called "residual," which literally means what remains after the greater part has gone. What remained of Rigsby's leg after the greater part was gone due to the accident was not worth saving; not physically and not in terms of his spiritual well being either.

He was tired of being a "professional patient" and wanted to get on with his life, so after 17 surgeries, he had to make an extremely tough decision, he told doctors to remove the leg.

I began this chapter with Scott's story, because it, in some way, is all of our story. We all get caught lingering in a place where we should've been passing through. A leg, no doubt, is harder to part with than most of the little things we all hold onto in life, but neither is trivial. Big or small, the ability to move with conviction is an essential part of God's Word. Not to mention, it was the same dilemma addressed in the Old Testament when the Israelites were asking themselves in the desert, what are we doing here? They were lingering between where they'd been (Egypt) and where they wanted to be (Canaan).

EXODUS, MOVEMENT OF THE PEOPLE

Quitting, or giving up, doesn't just happen, it's a decision, just like running in the previous chapter was a decision. Scott Rigsby didn't quit when he told the doctors to cut off his leg, but rather he made a very difficult decision to move from a place of adversity to a place of promise. His is a modern day version, and very personal parallel, to the struggle and emotions of the Exodus story.

The promised land was a place God told Moses to lead his people to, where crops would grow, families would be safe and where prosperity would be abundant. All they had to do was to trust in the Lord's Word and keep moving.

That is all we are asked to do. Every day people wake up to a place of doubt, a place where they resist moving and second guess taking action that will lead them closer to where God wants them to be. It's never obvious or easy, and specifically in this case, nobody says, without hesitation, yea, cut off my leg, that's what God wants. But let's be realistic, there is always a struggle, a time of trial, when we are tested by fire. What I'm asking you to remember is that there is a journey that God has placed you on, and when you, in turn, place your faith in Him, then he will direct your steps, be it writing a book or running a triathlon.

Where we go wrong is when we fail to realize we're being held captive to our own indecision, imprisoning ourselves in a place that we've created out of fear to move. When something locks us up and keeps us from moving, we become paralyzed, only seeing problems. In the case of the Israelites, they were physically afraid as they'd heard stories of giants waiting for them in Canaan. This caused them to focus on fear, saying, "if only we had died in Egypt...wouldn't it be better for us to return there...Let's choose a new leader and go back."

It's difficult not to sympathize with the plight of anybody leaving their hometown and the life they knew behind, but the greatest lesson in the Exodus story is that before the Israelites could even get to their new destination, restlessness and bitterness had won them over. They lost sight of the promises God made to them and they became grumpy, they argued, but more than anything, they lacked the faith and discipline to remain focused.

This is extremely common to our human nature. We leave a bad situation and the going gets tough, so we begin to exaggerate the obstacles and suddenly the prior life doesn't seem so bad. It's the enemy's assault on our ability to persevere in tough times and for the spiritually unprepared, it's often the difference between stagnation and progress, success and failure, even life and death.

Christian author Warren Wiersbe says: *"Nothing paralyzes our lives like the attitude that things can never change. We need to remind ourselves that God can change things. Outlook determines outcome. If we see only the problems, we will be defeated; but if we see the possibilities in the problems, we can have victory."*

DO YOU FEEL LIKE I DO

The strength to persevere when challenges arise and circumstances seem bleak is one of the most spoken about elements of human performance. From business to sports to politics, the power to move forward in the face of adversity is one of the most critical to success.

When one member of a team or family starts to get pessimistic, it can easily infect others. When the Jewish people experienced a little trepidation, they did what we all might do, they said they would just camp out and lay low for a few days until they could regroup. After all, they'd been through a lot and were tired. What happened next is another trap of human nature, they became stagnant, unmotivated and discontent. In the simplest of terms you might relate to, they got comfortable being uncomfortable and comfort is the enemy of progress. Rather than (tsalach) push forward, they hunkered down, turning what was to be a four day journey into 40 years of lingering.

A real life example I can give you from experience is this; when I was in my twenties, I came home from college and under a bit of pressure from my parents, took the first job I could find, which was selling pagers (don't laugh). Now nobody goes through four (maybe five) years of college to be a beeper salesman. It certainly wasn't my vision, but I needed the money. I specifically remember telling myself, when I took the job, David, no more than six months, just to get on your feet.

Three years later I was still there. Why? Because I got comfortable. I went on cruise control and lingered too long in a place I should've been passing through.

God cannot steer something that isn't willing to move.

Enter Joshua into this discussion, a man chosen by God to take over for Moses. He was exactly the type of leader the exiles needed to get out of stagnation and into belief. I'd compare Joshua to be the type of leader many of us are looking for in our positions of authority right now, whether it's in business or the government. He was young, brave and obedient to God. The only thing he lacked was a bit of maturity.

Like some leaders today, his bravado was not well received, at one point the Israelites even wanted to stone him for some of the things he said. I'd consider that might be the primitive version of being canceled on social media. We don't like what you're saying so we will just throw stones.

Here is the important part and how you can benefit from his story. Regardless of your situation, you'll benefit from reading about

Joshua because the way in which he handled himself is a great lesson in leadership. He kept his wits about him, he remained focused on his assignment and didn't get lazy, he was always trying to grow in his wisdom. Furthermore, he didn't go running off to a different tribe to complain, he didn't set out in a different direction on his own, rather he stayed loyal to his mentor, Moses, and always showed reverence to both he and God. And because Joshua never doubted the Lord, he would be rewarded accordingly.

THEY MIGHT BE GIANTS

Fear, dare I say it's the most preached on subject at both churches and self development seminars. It's always been a powerful emotion to overcome and in much the same way, we find ourselves today lingering in the sand and dust of the desert, eagerly looking for fruitful land to build, yet lacking the courage and faith to claim it. We've seen the masses of people over the last several years, believers among them, acting like the exiles of Israel, allowing fear and doubt to overcome them.

What's the one thing that we're not using enough of to help us overcome these fears? Certainly not more cable news or more government advice.

The Holy Spirit.

When a man or woman pushes away the noise of the world and surrounds themselves in a quiet peace, opening their arms to enthusiastically welcome in the Holy Ghost, everything changes.

After suffering on the cross and rising from the dead, Jesus returned to break bread with the Apostles, telling them to go to Jerusalem and await the "GIFT." The gift he spoke of was the Holy Spirit. It's been called the helper, the advocate, the intercessor, and yet so many people don't know about it. Paul reminds us, **where the Spirit is, there is freedom."** (2 Corinthians 3:17). That's exactly what so many are desperately seeking now, freedom. Freedom to make strong decisions and to take decisive action. Very few will enter into the fullness of the life in which they were called because they're unaware of how to access the Holy Spirit and therefore fearful of how to face off against the giants of our time; comparison, blame, self-doubt, fear, distraction, oppression and cancel culture.

Trust is a huge part of that equation. When we hear God say *I have a better plan for you*, it's not always an instant change, remember that. Joshua was more than patient when his nature might have been otherwise. He's a terrific example of faith and patience. Earlier, when I said you might have abandoned your faith walk because your prayers weren't answered when you wanted them to be, you have to remember sometimes you're going to wrestle with God like Jacob did in the Bible, meaning you're gonna have to do more than genuflect and make the sign of the cross. You're going to have to take your case to the cross.

The desert of the exiles was literal, but each of us has our own metaphorical desert we're lingering in. Case in point, if we go back to Scott Rigsby's day of reckoning, he had to take his case to the cross. After enduring 11 years of wondering in a desert of physical pain and stagnation, he says it all came to a head one day when he finally had his wrestle with his maker;

"I'd never condone the way I spoke to God, and trust me, I've repented for it," Rigsby said. "But God wasn't condemning me. In His gentle, loving fatherly way, He said 'I'm glad you're finally being honest with me. You're finally seeking a relationship with me...

It was as clear as can be, there was like a loud clap of His hands in heaven, like God was calling his angels over saying 'look at this one, this is the one I'm gonna use. He is finally being honest with me."

That's a powerful statement! Perhaps you've wrestled with God or in the middle of it right now. Like any healthy relationship, when you're tired and at the end of your rope, physically and mentally, it's then that you finally surrender. It's at that moment when you can be transparent and honest with him, when you truly seek relationship.

DO YOU KNOW WHERE YOU'RE GOING TO?

Retrospection is a part of life, we all pause every now and again to evaluate where we are and where we're going. We do a progress report or "motive check" like John Maxwell said of Jonah. We ask ourselves, is this where I'm meant to be and if not, what's my next move? It reminds me of the theme song to Mahogany by Motown legend Diana Ross which goes; *Do You Know where you're going to? Do you like the things that life is showing you?*

This stage of life can be extremely tough. I know because I ask this exact question (do you know where you're going to) to the people I coach, and guess what, most don't, they can only say they no longer want to stay where they are. Many are just like Ross' character in the movie, they're evaluating life's journey, where they've already been and what possibilities lie ahead, ultimately coming to a familiar realization; what we often thought would bring us joy, may look completely different or just harder to obtain than we anticipated.

My first goal is to encourage them to reconnect with God, to seek the Holy Spirit as a guide. Because our modern world seeks comfort, because we're often encouraged to take the path of least resistance and because we're constantly being persuaded that man knows what's best for us, and that the supernatural doesn't exist, it's easy to miss the Spirit. Those who yield earthly influence, those who seek to have dominion over us, want us in agreement with what they say rather than in agreement with what God says.

Dr. Ralph F. Wilson put it this way;

When we're too comfortable with things in our lives, or perhaps have accepted the compromises for too long, it's difficult to make the changes necessary to re-align ourselves with God's will. We need change and the uncertainty that goes with it to become re-dependent upon God. And that is certainly what the people need at this point.

It's not hard to see that people are walking around lost, searching for leadership and direction. On the front cover of my Speak Up workbook it reads, *Connection, Conviction and Courage* as my course is modeled after the very same attributes Joshua possessed. These qualities are universal and they transcend time. They are three things I believe are in high demand today but rarely found.

This brings me to the final point concerning Joshua, he was no quitter. One thing that really baffles me when I address people concerning their goals in life, be it their business or their marriage, is when they say "I'm not thinking about quitting or giving up" to which my answer is always "of course not, who mentioned anything about quitting? Why would that even come out of your mouth?" Take quitting off the table as an option and watch how your life changes.

In my experience, quitting is not just second guessing yourself, it's second guessing the one who made all of this, the world. Just because somewhere along the way your spirit was crushed by somebody or the thoughts of the world got into your head, doesn't mean it's time to quit. Quitting is a decision to stop trying. Quitting is a giving up on hope and that's were the Israelites failed miserably.

They decided to wait. And wait. And wait. The problem here isn't so much indecision, that's human nature to a great degree, the problem is in recognizing our idleness and not waking up to do something about it. Faith and momentum work so well in conjunction with one another but when one is lacking, the results are often lackluster, even disastrous.

I remember my days as a newspaper journalist, interviewing a man who had just climbed Mount Everest. He spoke of peering out of his binoculars as they set up camp late one afternoon. In the distance, gazing up toward the ridge, he witnessed a hiker stop and sit down. He knew from experience that at that altitude, which they call the "death zone," sitting for too long can be bad, even fatal. At that elevation it's cold and windy and there is only about a third of the oxygen, so if you are moving too slowly, your oxygen will run out.

The man told me that when he came out of his tent the next morning, he again took out his binoculars and gazed in the same direction. The hiker was sitting in that same position and he'd come to the grim reality that the man had frozen to death in that spot.

In this case, lingering too long in a frozen wilderness where one can easily run out of oxygen (breath) was deadly to the physical body. In your case, lingering too long in a spiritual wilderness when you can run out of oxygen (ruach) can be deadly to your spirit. If you don't like where you are going to and you sit too long, one day you will look around and time will have passed you by. The devil is in the delay. So, if it's more time with your children, don't sit. If it's repairing your marriage, don't sit. If it's chasing down or becoming something you've always dreamed of, don't sit. Get after it!

TO BEE OR NOT TO BEE?

So I have come down to deliver them from the power of the Egyptians,
and to bring them up from that land to a good and spacious land,
to a land flowing with milk and honey

First mentioned in Exodus 3:8 (above), the land of milk and honey is Canaan, a lush area between the Mediterranean Sea and the Jordan River where God promised his people they could grow and thrive. Think about that, milk and honey, made by cows and bees, two animals who throughout history, since the beginning of time, have always contributed a great deal to feeding us and to our health.

Milk and honey are two of the most nutrient dense substances in nature, but have you considered this, that the cows and the bees do most of the work for us in producing the food. We just gather or harvest it. Can't the same be said for us in terms of prosperity in life? God's done the work, just look at the complexity of the human anatomy. He's crafted us with legs to walk, arms to work and minds to create. We have the ability to talk in a complex language like no other animal on earth and we possess an imagination to design things and generate amazing technology. He's given us gifts to succeed, all we have to do figure out is how to harvest them.

In homeschooling my children, I teach them about a different animal or insect every week and when it came to the bee, wow, did I learn a lot. For instance, to make just one tablespoon of honey, a bee has to visit 4,200 flowers. Each bee has 170 odorant receptors and bees beat their wings 200 times per second! But the most fascinating thing of all that I learned is that all bees do what's called a "waggle dance." These amazing creations of God do a dance to tell other bees the precise location of flowers, in both direction and distance, as to how to find honey - specifically in terms of what angle the flower is from the sun and how far the flower is from the hive. It's been deemed "the dance that sustains life."

Isn't it amazing that bees communicate to alert other bees to where to find food to sustain life much the same as the Word of God communicates where to find food to sustain the spirit?

I recall my oldest daughter listening to me tell her how hard the bees work and asked me "Dad, how much longer will I have to go to school?"

I said about 11 years and then she asked "then I get to go to work like the bees?"

I laughed and said yes. And her last comment was "good, there are a lot of places I want to go and a lot of things I want to accomplish."

At six, my daughter was already envisioning two very important motivators, freedom and legacy. It is exactly what the people of Israel were craving when they followed Moses out of Egypt. However they lingered in the desert for forty years because they were missing the most critical element to prosperity - ambition.

We're living in a time when the doors of opportunity have been swung wide open and my daughter Ella's generation already sees, wants and expects way more out of life than her grandparents or even I have experienced. But we must instill in our children that freedom and legacy don't exist without ambition. Angelike and I have felt like the Israelites plenty of times in different seasons of our lives. We've looked at one another and felt like quitting. There were other times when we pitied ourselves, looking up to the sky and having that tough conversation saying "God, we're trying to do everything you told us to do, but we're not seeing the promised land." And yes, there were times when we just wanted to pout and complain and take a rest.

Frustrated - Who do we think we are. We can't do this.

Fearful - Where are we headed? What if there are giants there?

Stagnant - We should just stop and rest. This is good enough.

These were the thoughts holding us back, and what had the secular gods taught us? Pound your chest and yell. Tell yourself your good enough. Follow my steps. It was more like going to a Rocky movie, the old repeated cliche *when the going gets tough, the tough get going.* But when you've done that so much, at some point it all just becomes inspirational entertainment. We can talk ourselves out of something just as quickly as we said we could do it when our thoughts and actions aren't grounded in a foundation of love and truth, when we're not reminded that we are the sons and daughters of a royal bloodline.

Weighty decisions in life will never go away, in fact they just get bigger. There's nothing wrong with a motivational speech from a knowledge teacher, but when we need to be convicted in spirit in order to break through deep wounds and limitations, again, knowledge only goes so far. That is why we can gobble up self help books that regurgitate the same platitudes by different authors and still not experience growth or transformation. It's why you have a room full of thousands of people convinced they will change but only a handful do. Their minds says yes, they want the milk and honey, but their spirits have not changed. Their foundation is still that they are alone, without the helper, advocate or intercessor we know as the Holy Spirit. This brings us back to Joshua and one of the hardest lessons of this story - there is no reward for the lukewarm.

WE ARE THE CHAMPIONS

God was not very happy with Moses or the Israelites. As a result, he said that their generation would not see the promised land, proving the point that waiting or disobeying God when He tells you to proceed can be a costly error. He will not reward doubt and complacency.

Be it crossing the Jordan River or crossing into a new job or new marriage, there is nothing that hurts more than giving up only to find out victory was right around the corner or that had you given just a little more effort, you would have received the reward. It's why Paul reminds us to finish our race and why I remind you that now is the time for strong God-centered leadership, not bickering, in the places and situations where the devil is trying to divide and conquer. When we see strong churches and strong marriages falling apart or anointed pastors and good business leaders falling victim to temptation and corruption, it's a clear sign that we're under a spiritual attack and we need to step up our commitments.

The world is in need of more Joshuas.

What's the alternative if we don't? Are we, the Body of Christ, just going to sit around in indecision, in this metaphorical desert, stagnant and complaining because we have a fear of being canceled? Are we going to point fingers at one another and throw a pity party blaming everything but ourselves for why the world is getting darker and more corrupt? History is always repeating itself and what's happening now is exactly what kept the Jewish exiles in a holding pattern. There just aren't enough people willing to **SPEAK UP** and lead like Joshua. In Numbers 14:9 when the other men are frightened and hesitant to go into Canaan, Joshua gives two commands; do not rebel against the Lord and do not be afraid of the people in the land.

Devotion and bravery, that is what God has, and still is, demanding of His leaders. Remember when I spoke about "just because" not being a good answer to the question *WHY* we should believe? What about when it comes to the question of what qualifies us to lead? John C. Maxwell says that *every leader must remember that people subconsciously ask why should I listen to you?* Whether you run a business or a team or a family, your leadership ability will be questioned.

Allow me to bridge between the Old and New Testament, going from old leader (Joshua) to new (Simon Peter), so that you might be able to cement a clear picture of how to model Christian leadership.

Simon Peter was Christ's most spirited and outspoken disciple. When his team (countrymen) or family (fellow disciples) looked to him for strength, he was forthright, saying to his followers that even though you're aware of the message, it's my job to keep telling you over and over, to make every effort to add wisdom and be careful not to stumble. He said to them, because the stakes are so high and the world so corrupt, as long as I live, I will not let up for a minute.

Doesn't our world call for this type of conviction right now? When you lead, you will be asked the same questions Simon Peter was asked; *Why are we doing this, Why should we believe in you as a leader and in Jesus as the Messiah?* He answers by reminding them that he was an eyewitness and saw it first hand. He says, we (the disciples) weren't making this stuff up about Jesus Christ. We were there when he was resurrected.

Do we need to have been there to feel this convicted in our spirit? If you know God, speak to God and feel him, isn't your answer just as valid? You should draw strength just by looking in the mirror at the miracle in front of you. Look into your own eyes with all their millions of moving parts and address any lingering fear that might be hiding. Face it head on. In doing that you kickstart your own revival and get out of stagnation. Simon Peter said to the people, because I know how easy it is to get distracted, to become discouraged and let our guard down, I'll repeat this message of Jesus Christ and continue to remind you of his love and instructions until the day I die.

As a husband, father and business owner, living in times which seem to be so chaotic, I'll remind you right now, HE IS RISEN! That's why we do what we do. That's why we persist in the desert and ask God to place our steps. If you are not in the ear of other believers and if we aren't constantly pouring belief into our children, then who will? The enemy! His goal is to negate the Word. He whispers in the ears of doubters, of people facing giants, that you can't go there. He tells you that you're not strong enough, smart enough or brave enough. You're a failure. Turn around and go home.

"If I were your enemy, I'd constantly remind you of your past mistakes and poor choices. I'd want to keep you burdened by shame and guilt, in hopes that you'll feel incapacitated by your many failings and see no point in even trying again. I'd work to convince you that you've had your chance and blown it.
- Priscilla Shirer

How will you lead, in fear in or in fortitude? That's not intended to be a feel-good fist pumping question, it's more of a motive check that you need a real answer to. Will you allow your social media profile to define you with airbrushed photos and regurgitated platitudes on a color palette or will you say I may not have a perfect past or perfect body, but I strive to have a perfect heart.

What does your walk through life look like? Scott Rigsby told me, very literally, he was worried about how the world would perceive him, a man who had no legs. Would he be looked upon with shame or pity as half a man who was less than perfect physically? He sat in that place for some time, but came to a point where he was tired of lingering in fear or what might be and instead he got up and took control of his future. I know it's not easy, we're all carrying baggage, some fear, some hurt, some, just a streak of bad luck. Rigsby's story speaks to all of that, he says he had to come to a place where he *refused to be defined by a physical part of me.*

> *"I tell people not to lose hope and to continue to find God's purpose for their lives, that he can take whatever is left and make things greater than the whole. You can do that in God's economy. It's the only one in the world where you can take something from somebody that's perceived as a weakness, and yet the divine result is exponentially greater than the whole."*

I WILL SURVIVE

Resolve is the ability "to decide firmly on a course of action." And if I were interviewing job candidates, this would be very high on my list of things I'd be looking for. In layman's terms it means "to show grit" or "to have a backbone". You have to be able to take a punch on the chin, dust yourself off and get back in there. I believe in mentorship and modeling but at some point, in all of our lives, be it in a big way or small, we need to define resolve for ourselves (by means of the Holy Spirit) and stop relying on coaches to prop us up.

The start of this new decade brought more confusion and transition than any other time most of us can remember. Some moved careers, some moved cities and some moved mountains. But some didn't move at all, even when they needed to. Why?

It's an important question, and the quick and easy answer is uncertainty. The fear of the unknown has always preyed upon man's ability to move confidently in a direction. The exiles fleeing Egypt were terrifed by a man, the Pharaoh. It's understandable, and it's why many people have relinquished their power over to earthly authority to this day. We're convinced we're too weak to make our own decisions, so we seek Big Government or Big Pharma to keep us safe in these uncertain times. If you promise to protect me, in return, I'll do whatever you ask of me, even if it means giving up my God given rights.

I ask my clients to look in the mirror and ask themselves what more conviction and more courage to claim autonomy over their own lives would feel like. I say seek Godly intuition or discernment, not the flawed ideas of government leaders and celebrities. They're human just like us, so when you say something that goes against your gut instinct, run it through the filter of the Bible.

There is absolutely zero doubt in my mind that there's been a very calculated move to intercept the direct line of communication between God and his sons and daughters which can only come through prayer and the wisdom of the Word. It's nothing new, in fact it was a staple of the reformation. Martin Luther questioend why he would need a third party to communicate with the almighty God or why one would have to pay out of pocket for salvation when the Word tells us it is by grace that we are saved.

Jesus said give to Caesar the things that are Caesar's, meaning taxes basically. But for all other things, come to who? The Father!

Seek and you will find. Pray to me and seek my face. Cast your anxieties upon me. I (God) will give you rest. I (God) will give you shelter.

Isn't it obvious how man, in his lust for power and dominion, has intercepted all of those scriptures and attempted to insert him or herself in God's place. The leaders of the Protestant Reformation witnessed this same power grab, one of organized religion in concert with the state, or in those days, the emperors. Look upon their words of the past and pretend they were written yesterday to see how long this fight has been going on and how these truths are even more relevant in our time.

"The gospel alone is sufficient to rule the lives of Christians everywhere - any additional rules made to govern men's conduct added nothing to the perfection already found in the Gospel of Jesus Christ."
-John Wycliffe

"I am afraid that the schools will prove the very gates of hell, unless they diligently labor in explaining the Holy Scriptures and engraving them in the heart of the youth."
- Martin Luther

"Our confidence in Christ does not make us lazy, negligent, or careless, but on the contrary it awakens us, urges us on, and makes us active in living righteous lives and doing good. There is no self-confidence to compare with this."
-Ulrich Zwingli

"The surest source of destruction to men is to obey themselves."
- John Calvin

The offices and the authorities which disseminate information to the public have, little by little, over the gradual road, edged out God's authority and assumed more for themselves. It's the power grab that mankind cannot seem to avoid. It reoccurs over and over, again and again, and it can only be described as the ongoing earthly battle between God and his fallen angel - man's rebellion against his maker and the Creator's desire to restore the relationship.

It can feel quite heavy, especially for those who are unfamiliar with Bible prophecy and how beautifully intricate the Old and New

Testament are woven. So let's dumb is down for the sake of making it easier to move out of the desert and into our own land of milk and honey, *Did you get what you're hoping for*? That is my favorite question when it comes to putting any faith in earthly authority. Did they balance that budget they promised or is it growing? Did they refrain from pouring on more taxes or engaging in more wars? Did they protect you from fear and pestilence?

When people drift from the Word of God and experiment with taking their lead from man, in the form of government or false idols, it's easy to look back at the decisions and give a clear yes or no as to whether there was fruit from that decision.

Moses sent twelve spies into the promised land and when they returned with discouraging words of fear and giants, man forgot what God said. Or a better choice of words would be, they chose to ignore what God said.

There were repercussions for them.

We're never meant to rush things. There is always a time to be still. But I want you to remember, when the situation arises in your life when you feel stuck or when you know you're lingering, to recall the story of the Israelites in the desert and use this story as a reminder to yourself to keep moving in faith, because in the end, God always rewards thouse who are obedient. Because of their faith, Joshua and Caleb entered Canaan and were rewarded.

DID YOU KNOW

Prior to 1896, there was very little evidence outside of the Bible to substantiate that the Israelites and Egyptians ever interacted with one another.

In what's known as one of the most important archaeological discoveries in Biblical history, that changed. In 1896 Sir William Flinders Petrie, an English Egyptologist/archaeologist, found a ten-foot-tall black granite slab (a stele or stela) in the ruins of the funerary temple of Pharaoh Merenptah.

Now housed in the Cairo Museum, this victory slate which boasts of Egyptian war triumphs, provides powerful evidence that a people who called themselves Israelites were living in Canaan at the time of the Egyptian emperor.

The hieroglyphic text on the stele contained the first and only known ancient Egyptian reference to the people of Israel, reading **"Israel has been shorn. Its seed no longer exists."** The mention indicates that the Israelites must have been considerable in number and somewhat formidable or they would not have warranted mention. Merenptah claims to have violently suppressed God's chosen people, but we know that is not true.

CHAPTER 15

YOU PLAY TO WIN THE GAME

Prayer is life passionately wanting, wishing,
desiring God's triumph. Prayer is life striving and toiling
everywhere and always for that ultimate victory.
- G. Campbell Morgan

This final chapter is the story of King Joash, an obscure couple of paragraphs tucked away in the book of Kings concerning a rather meager ruler who you've probably never heard of before.

So why save it for last then? What deems this worthy to be the closer? I've saved it for last because in some small, or quite possibility large way, it's a part of all of our stories. A part that we're missing. In fact, I'd be willing to guarantee that this story of King Joash directly relates to something that you're struggling with or trying to accomplish right now.

Joash was the twelfth King of Israel and reigned 16 years (798–782 BC). By no means was he considered a great leader or a great man of the Bible because while he outwardly worshiped God, his devotion was feigned because he still allowed the worship of false idols.

As scripture goes, the Syrian army was invading Israel and King Joash, in a panic, sought the counsel of Elisha, a great prophet, and successor to Elijah. At the time, Elisha was on his deathbed, but nonetheless advises Joash, saying *"Get a bow and some arrows and open the east window and shoot The Lord's arrow of victory....You will completely destroy the Arameans at Aphek....take the arrows and strike the ground."*

At this command Joash took the arrows, opened the window and struck the ground, but only three times. Elisha became very angry and said *"You should have struck the ground five or six times; then you would have defeated Aram and completely destroyed it. But now you will defeat it only three times."*

At first glance, the story may seem a bit confusing or lackluster. He shot an arrow three times instead of five. Big deal? You said this is a story that is gonna change my life?

The very powerful lesson I need you to take from this is, when we *hold back*, when we don't use our full arsenal of weapons, particularly after getting a Word from God, the outcome is not good. That's the message, plain and simple.

Of these three reasons, running, lingering and holding back, it always seems to be running or lingering that make up an overwhelming majority of the answers people give as to why they are not progressing, but I beg to differ and say that a majority of the time, it's the third reason. We're just playing it safe, failing to empty our efforts (our talent) God gifted us with in order to succeed. As a consequence, we hold ourselves back from fulfilling our greatest potential. When you run from something or wait for something, it's almost understandable, you never really had it, so you might be able to live with the guilt, but to have victory right there in your sights, and miss out on it because you thought you'd play it safe and not take God at his word? That's gonna leave a mark.

RATTLE AND HUM

We all get our cage rattled at some point. I think it's safe to say the world is experiencing some major cage rattling right now. If we look to the Word for wisdom we see that God gave the children of Israel (Jacob) the promised land (milk and honey), but they still had to fight to procure it for themselves. In my opinion, I don't think God wants us to sit in the prone position and wait for victory, we must contend for it. It goes with the spiritual prosperity of *tsalach* in Jeremiah 29:11. God told His people they would be okay but they had to fight through some tough days ahead, just like we are now.

The Israelites under Joshua were given the promised land but they had to fight for every acre including Jericho, the most fortified city in the world at that time. The fight doesn't always look the same. Remember this is a messaging war were in. The weapons look different. In the ancient days they used arrows and sometimes even horns, meaning how did Joshua take Jericho, not with swords but with the hum of the rams trumpets. The method or weaponry may change but the message remains the same, the walls of the most fortified city in the world fell down because they followed God's instructions to a T, even though they must've seemed counterintuitive at the time.

The Lord said to Joshua, "Look. I have given Jericho and its king into your power, along with its mighty warriors. Circle

the city with all the soldiers, going around the city one time.
Do this for six days. Have seven priests carry seven trumpets
made from rams' horns in front of the chest. On the seventh
day, circle the city seven times, with the priests
blowing the trumpets.
"Have them blow a long blast on the ram's horn. As soon as
you hear that trumpet blast, have all the people shout out a
loud war cry. Then the city wall will collapse.
Joshua 6: 2-6

That was the gameplan and Joshua executed it. Joash, did not execute it. He left arrows on the table. The lesson is, never give half of what you're commanded to give. This happens every day in life, we get convitcted to take action, we get confirmation from above, but then the enemy whispers in our ear..*but what if*.. and then we second guess the Word of God "just in case." Going back to chapter 10, this is what "playing small" looks like.

Ecclesiastes 9:10 says **Whatever your hand finds to do, do it with all your might** be it a battle for your marriage, for your livelihood or for your freedom. Nineteenth century poet R.H. Stoddard echoed the above scripture writing **All that you do, do with your might. Things done by halves are never done right.** Of all the lessons in the Bible, this is the one I chose to bat cleanup because I feel like the people or forces that influence our culture have done such a good job at separating us from direct connection with the Lord and thereby convincing us that we are weak. It's alright to be afraid when we face danger or obstacles, but what does the Word tell us to focus on in the eye of the storm? Jesus!

Remember back in chapter 11, Jacob was rewarded for his ambition. He esteemed to have his father's birthright so bad that he wrestled with an angel the entire night through. Even when he dislocated his hip he kept fighting, saying to the angel, *"You can't go until you bless me."*

"What is your name?" asked the angel.

"Jacob," he answered.

The angel said, "Your name will no longer be Jacob. You have wrestled with God and with men, and you have won. That's why your name will be Israel."

Jacob became Israel, in man and nation, showing us that in order to be prosperous, we must treasure God's blessing and then follow through on it.

EASY LIKE SUNDAY MORNING

On any given Sunday, 46 modern day warriors suit up to face 46 opponents. It's about as competitive of an environment as you'll come by. As a sports journalist, I've been in a lot of NFL locker rooms and let me tell you, it's never a good feeling being in the losing locker room of men who live to compete. But do you know what's worse? Being in a locker room of a team that had victory all but locked up only to have it snatched away at the last second.

It was 2003, but I remember it like it was yesterday. Players with fury in their eyes punching walls and throwing helmets. Hands down, I've never been as unnerved at any moment of my career as I was that Monday night in Tampa Bay. It's on the NFL's 100 Greatest Games list

(No. 65), but it wasn't so great for the Buccaneers as The Indianapolis Colts became the first team in NFL history to win after trailing by 21 or more points with less than four minutes to play in regulation.

I use this game as an example because I feel like sport is such a great metaphor for life. It wasn't losing that night that was so tragic, nobody wants to lose, but it's part of the game. It was how they lost. When victory is so close you can taste it, but you let apathy, or a failure to finish the job, steal it from you, it can be devastating. Sometimes you don't recover. That was the case with Bucs. It was just the fourth game of the season for reigning world champs, having won the franchise's first Super Bowl eight months prior, but they would never recover. Jon Gruden's team lost four of their next six games and missed the playoffs.

Wake up! Strengthen what remains and is about to die.
Revelations 3:2

If you are fighting for your marriage, fighting for your paycheck or fighting for your country, God is telling you to empty the tank, don't let up. Not now, not when you are so close to victory. I tell you to fight in this, the final chapter of the book, but I only repeat what I've learned from the final book of the Bible.

I've had many good coaches but I have one God. In this verse He tells us, the one who is worthy, who is victorious, will be remembered and acknowledged before my Father. So many good people will fall away at the last moment, they will have victory in their grasp but get lazy and lose sight of what's at stake.

Do not take your eyes off of victory!

Tony Dungy, who was in the winning locker room that night in 2003, said "They never gave up, that is what I like about us. I had a feeling that the Lord was going to do something special today, and he certainly did."

Now while I've never thought that God picks and chooses winners in sports, I love that Coach Dungy always acknowledged which fight was the most important. That's the fight we're in right now, one for the defense of God's Word and for our salvation. In his book *Quiet Strength: The Principles, Practices & Priorities of a Winning Life,* Dungy writes;

"I love coaching football, and winning a Super Bowl was a goal I've had for a long time. But it has never been my purpose in life. My purpose in life is simply to glorify God."

KNOW THE GOAL

I spent many Sundays of my life taking notes on why one team won and the other didn't. I've heard all the speeches and wrote down all the cliches, but there is one in particular that stands out. While I wasn't in the room to hear it live, its always resonated with me and has become a soundbite which I play for all my classes that are filled with hungry entrepreneurs trying to win. It's of former New York Jets coach Herm Edwards who, after a particularly disappointing loss, was asked by a New York Times reporter "Do you have to talk to your team about not giving up on the season?

Edwards' response, which would end up going viral, was, "**HELLO, you play to win the game. This is the greatest thing about sports, you play to win the game.**"

At the time, (October 2002) the Jets had just suffered a devastating loss and fell to 2-5, but the fiery and very blunt speech was a wakeup call to his team, it was exactly what they needed, and the Jets went on to win seven of their next nine games, even winning a playoff game over Peyton Manning's Colts 41-0.

Years later, when interviewed about his famous comment, Edwards said "don't forget the Hello!"

I'm reiterating that now. **HELLO!** as in, knock-knock, this is a wake up call for you to turn your season around and start playing to win the game.

You play to win the game!

Whether you're going into work stressing about hitting your numbers or stepping into the batter's box in the World Series, the message in God's Word is clear, never give a check swing. He tells us to swing for the fences. Swing away in the face of overwhelm. Swing away despite urges to self sabotage. Swing away even when fear tugs on your sleeve telling you "but, just in case" or "that's good enough."

When you can begin to embrace the concept that so much of what happens in life comes down to faith and taking action, then you allow yourself to tap into a level of co-creation you never thought possible.

TAKE ME BACK TO CHURCH

Way before Sundays were synonymous with football, there was this little thing called church and one Sunday morning in April 1893, one of its most valuable players, the great evangelist Charles Spurgeon, stood up in front of his congregation and began his message by saying:

It is a very difficult task to show the meeting place of the purpose of God and the free agency of man....It is also a sure and certain fact that, oftentimes, events hang upon the choice of men. Their will has a singular potency. In the case before us, the arrows are in the hands of the King of Israel.

That's right, the term *free agency* existed way before football did, but how interesting that Sprugeon references the intersection of God's purpose and our free will as the centerpiece of his sermon on King Joash. Free will has been a centerpiece of this book.

Do me a favor and go to that intersection right now, meaning your own personal experience. When have you and God come to a crossroad? When have you paused, knowing that you received a sign or a nudge directing you, but your free will, or freedom to doubt in this case, provided a number of excuses to ignore his orders and give half of your effort, you know, just in case God might be wrong.

Do I have to point out the sarcasm? Hello!! You play to win the game and therefore it's never good to ignore the signs, or even nudges. The question is, why do we miss them? Spurgeon, being very intune with human nature, gives us two of the biggest reasons, the first being *the fear of being too holy.* In the 1800s it was worded: *are you afraid of being presumptuous?*

This looks like how we, as Christians, often worry about how we will be judged by culture when we take a stance for God. It's a hesitation that can easily cloud our decision to take action. I've heard, dumb it down, just say "Love" because some people don't want to hear about God. I've heard dumb it down, say God but include *whatever you believe* as well. I've heard dumb it down, the name Jesus is too polarizing for some people.

It's a no-win situation that I spoke of earlier. You're going to offend culture or offend God. Which will it be?

God isn't looking for fence-sitters, He wants hands waving saying here I am, send me. What I can tell you from experience is that when you're torn between if *I take too strong of a stance I look like I'm idolizing myself* and *don't speak up because you feel intimidated,* the answer is always to just be yourself, say what comes naturally, what your spirit is telling you to say. You cannot go wrong when you listen to your heart and when you speak according to the Holy Spirit.

I didn't want to halfway make it to heaven, so I decided I wasn't going to water down my message. I knew it might not be perfect, but on the other hand I wasn't about to pre-apoligize if I made an error or if I said something that might challenge somebody. I wrote this book doing my best, giving my all, at great sacrifice to my family who watched me struggle.

And I'm not saying that on a soap box, looking for pats on the back from other believers, but many people will tell you to hold back and play it safe when it comes to shooting your arrows. This book was my Joash moment. We're all gonna have our Joash moment, where we sit there and look around thinking, sure this is what God is telling me to do, but I live in this world, maybe I can do half of what he says and play it safe (please the world) and with the other half I'll please God.

In writing my copy for my courses, I would get that feeling, I'd be ready to put them online and I'd pause, telling myself, "awe that's too much scripture." Even during the writing of this book, I'd want to soften up some points to make it more palpable for a larger audience, asking myself "are you going too God heavy?"

Then one day it hit me, David, you're writing a chapter about holding back your arrows and questioning God's Word and you're telling yourself you're being too intense, too Jesus heavy? That doesn't make any sense, practice what you're preaching, your maker created you to shine light, not dim it. Like Matthew said, don't put your lamp under a bowl. Instead, put it on a stand to give light to others.

Spurgeon continues, saying another reason we hold back our arrows is because we're afraid of asking for too much help from God, or we feel unworthy. Whether you've been engaged in what you've perceived as unforgivable sin or you're just incredibly humble, when you play small with God, you get small returns. Again, His purpose and our free will are at a crossroads, accept all of His grace and shoot all your arrows with confidence or only obtain a partial blessing or small victory. Spurgeon says *There is no presumption in taking the largest promise of God and pleading it, and expecting to have it fulfilled.*

Isn't that beautiful? Take it all. He wants you to have the maximum blessing. But that's exactly what I was missing. It is what so many others I've talked to have been missing too. We fail to take

His promise. We fail to open the door and accept the gifts. But He wants you to have them. Think of it this way, as a father, when I give something to my children, I don't give something with the thought that I'm going to take it back or that I don't really want them to have it. It's always out of pure love that I give and in hopes that my children will take it and run with it. Our heavenly father's gives with the same love.

The other reasons Spurgeon gives as to why men and women "too soon pause" or "don't follow through" should be equally studied as they are just as relevant today as the day he spoke them in 1893

- I don't have the natural ability
- I am getting too old
- I'm too dependent upon other people
- I've done enough (my share)
- Too little zeal (lack passion).

Where can you plug in an excuse or two, maybe three, that's holding you back? When you take a reductionist approach to life, you say two things to God; (1) you're not really who you say you are. (2) I'm more than happy to be a tiny little candle rather than a flaming torch for the Kingdom.

FOR KING AND COUNTRY

*"It is but natural that the first paragraph of the Declaration
of Independence should open with a reference to Nature's God and
should close in the final paragraphs with an appeal to the Supreme
Judge of the world and an assertion of a firm reliance
on Divine Providence."*
- President Calvin Coolidge

In Washington D.C. circles, he was known as Silent Cal because he was a man of few words. One story goes that a man seated next to him at a dinner, said to him, "I made a bet today that I could get more than two words out of you." Coolidge replied, "You lose."

I mention him here because many consider his speech (quoted above), celebrating the 150th anniversary of the Declaration of Independence, the "gold standard" of Fourth of July Presidential addresses.

Let's be honest, Coolidge won't pop up on any of the "Greatest Presidents" lists but he was a man of conviction. He was a civil rights activist before his time, he supported women's suffrage before his time and he was a fiscal conservative whose economic policies ushered in the Roaring Twenties. Furthermore, he was not power hungry. He refused to run for a second term of office.

He may seem like an odd addition but I mention him to help sum up the critical part of the Joash story and shine a light on what I feel the world needs most right now, fortitude. Coolidge said *"Nothing in this world can take the place of persistence.*

Talent will not: nothing is more common
than unsuccessful men with talent.
Genius will not; unrewarded genius is almost a proverb.
Education will not: the world is full of educated derelicts.
Persistence and determination alone are omnipotent."

Not everybody will like what I'm about to say, but we need to get tough again. We need to stop making things easier, enabling people to sit and then reward sloth. Things done by half are never done right. We have talented actors and educated politicians but nothing trumps a persistent patriot or a determined mom or dad.

DO NOT MISS THIS, as you close this book, lock this into your memory and meditate on it, PROSPERITY IS AT THE INTERSECTION OF GOD'S PROMISES AND OUR FREE WILL. When you hear the command to shoot your arrows, use the gifts and talents God gave you and shoot everything you have with divine appointment. Hold back and you will lack.

And don't forget, it's never just about you. You fight for your family and for future generations. Jonah had a direct effect on the Ninivites, Joshua on the Israelites and Joash on an entire kingdom. Others will prosper or suffer because of your effort or lack of it.

We've been through the ringer the last few years. We've expressed every human emotion possible.

We've bared it ALL.

We've taken blow after blow.

We've knelt down. We've stood up. We've knelt down again.

But through it all, the one constant has been God's love for us and our love for Him and each other. When the world gets tough and loud and hurtful and distractions are high; you have a choice: to flip out or flip ON. Angelike and I have done both. But we know that to keep our gaze straight ahead we have to be Turned On even when it feels easiest to turn off.

With emotions at all time high, we still remember what's most important, God, and if we can simply keep our focus on Him, we cannot fail. He tells us whoever hears good things and shares will be given more. Whoever sows and scatters seeds will be fed. Don't sit on your gifts my friends, use them wisely to spread good and you will be rewarded.

If you're given a gift, don't hide it, don't put it under a bed, put it on a lamp stand.

GET TURNED ON. GET IN THE PURSUIT OF THE WORD